The Complete
Phonic Handbook

Diana Hope

The Complete Phonic Handbook

First published in 2001 by R.I.C. Publications
Republished 2002

American English version published in 2002 by R.I.C. Publications
Published in the United States and Canada by Didax Inc. – *info@didaxinc.com*
Distributed in Japan and Korea by Tuttle Publishing/Tuttle ELT – *tuttle@gol.com*

Copyright Diana Hope

R.I.C. Publications, PO Box 332, Greenwood WA 6924

Foreword

The Complete Phonic Handbook is an essential reference for all teachers responsible for the language development of young students. Presented in a format that will assist quick and easy reference, it features:

- notes on the development of grapho-phonic understanding;
- family word lists for grapho-phonic sounds, graded in levels of development;
- class activities to provide variety and interest to the teaching of grapho-phonics in the classroom. Color-coding is used throughout the book for ease of reference.

Contents

Introduction 1

Grapho-phonic Understanding/Explanation of Phonic Sounds Tables 2

Common Spellings for English Sounds: .... 3 – 4

How to Develop Grapho-phonic Understanding 5

Developmental Order of Grapho-phonic Understanding:

5 – 6 Reading Age 6

6 – 7 Reading Age 7

7 – 8 Reading Age 8

9 – 10 Reading Age .... 9 – 10

10+ Reading Age .... 13 – 14

11 – 12 Reading Age .... 15 – 17

Syllabification of Words 18

Grapho-phonic Family Word Lists 19

Explanation of Phonic Family Word Lists 20

- a; ai / a–e; ai; ay; a; ea; ey; ei; eigh; aigh; et; au 21
- are; air; ear; ere; eir; ayer / ar; a; ear; au; er 22
- b; bb / ch; tch; tu; ti; te 23
- d; dd; ed / e; a; ea; u; ie; ai; ay; eo; ae; ei 24
- ee; ea; y; ey; ie; i; e; ei; eo; ay; oe 25
- ir; er; ur; ear; or; our; yr / er; ar; ir; or; our; ur; yr; re; eur 26
- f; ff; gh; ph; ft; lf / g; gg; gh; gu; gue .. 27

- h; wh / i; E; o; u; ui; y; ie 28
- i – e; y; ie; i; igh; uy; ye; ei; ai; is / j; g; dge; gg; di 29
- c; k; ck; cc; ch; lk; cq; qu / l; ll 30
- m; mm; mb; lm; mn / n; nn; kn; gn; pn   31
- ng; ngue / o; a; ho; ou / oa; o – e; ow; o; oe; ough; ew; ear; eo; oo 32
- a; aw; or; au; oor; ore; oar; ough; augh
- ar; our / oi; oy; uoy 33
- ou; ow; ough / p; pp 34
- r; rr; wr; rh / s; ss; c; sc; ps; st 35
- h; ce; s; ci; si; sci; ch; ti / t; tt; th; ed / th/th; the / u; o; oo; ou 36
- oo; ou; u; o / oo; ew; oe; ue; ough; u; ui; o; ou; oeu / v; f; ph / w; wh; u; o 37
- x; cks / y; i; j / you; ew; iew; u; ue; you; eue; eu; eau; ieu / z; zz; s; ss; x / s; si; z; ge 38

Linking Consonant Word Lists

Initial Links 39

Final Links 40

Compound Word Lists 41

Greek and Latin Word Origin List 42

Class Activities for Use with Phonic Family Word Lists 43

Class Activities .... 44 – 56

Glossary of Terms 57

Introduction

Grapho-phonic Understanding

Grapho:	*prefix for "written".*
Phonology:	*the system of sounds used in a language; the study of sounds of a language.*
Phonetic:	*of or having to do with speech sounds; representing speech sounds; indicating pronunciation*
Awareness:	*knowing, realizing, being conscious of*

The grapho-phonic system provides information about letters and combinations of letters and the sounds associated with them. Successful grapho-phonic understanding results in rapid and accurate recognition and pronounciation of words.

The teacher's language program can assist students in the development of grapho-phonic understanding, enabling them to identify different sound patterns in words, first aurally and then visually.

In the English language there are 26 letters of the alphabet whose written symbols have letter names; but those same letters form about 44 sounds in the phonetic alphabet. If students are given the opportunity to become aware of these sounds aurally, and also develop the knowledge of the most common ways to spell these "sounds", they are able to use these "sounds" as a strategy when reading and spelling.

This awareness begins with students knowing single sounds (e.g., "a" – apple) and then progresses to their being aware of the different digraphs (e.g., "sh" – ship) and trigraphs (e.g., "air" – chair). This is a developmental process and the students will display a growing knowledge in personal daily writing, when they are given plenty of opportunity to attempt spelling words and subsequently read back their writing to themselves or to the class.

This book looks at some 240 different ways of spelling about 44 sounds, facilitating the development of grapho-phonic understanding over the years. Students will absorb knowledge at differing rates, so there is a need to be conscious of catering for individual differences.

Explanation of Phonic Sounds Tables

Listed on the next two pages are the different "sounds" made in words and the most common English spellings for these sounds.

- The first column has the phonetic alphabet symbol for the sound.

- The second and subsequent columns have lists of keywords showing different ways of representing these "sounds".

- The sound and keyword have been color-coded to correspond with the approximate reading age of the student. Initially, the student would (normally) be able to recognize the sound aurally and read it, before progressing to spelling it correctly.

Blue	**5, 6, 7 years**
Green	7, 8, 9, 10 years
Red	**10⁺ years**

Common Spellings for English Sounds

These are the different sounds made in words and the most common spellings for these sounds. Spelling can be a lot easier if words are grouped according to their "sound" families.

For easy reference, the table has been arranged alphabetically and color-coded for the different ages of reading/spelling development.

Symbol	Common Spellings of the Sound										
a	a hat and a	ai plaid	au laugh								
ā	a-e cake	ai rain	ay tray	a baby	ea break	ey they	ei vein	eigh weigh	aigh straight	et croquet	au gauge
ã	are care	air chair	ear pear	ere where	eir their	ayer prayer					
ä	ar car	ear heart	er sergeant								
b	b bat	bb rabbit									
ch	ch child	tch watch	tu future	ti question	te righteous						
d	d did	dd add	ed filled								
e	e let	a many	ea bread	u bury	ie friend	ai said	ay says	eo leopard	ae aesthetic	ei heifer	
ē	ee bee	ea leaf	y happy	ey key	ie chief	i ski and machine	e equal	ei receive	eo people	oe phoenix	
èr	ir first	er fern	ur church	ear pearl	or word	our journey	yr myrtle				
ər	er mother	ar liar	ir elixir	or doctor	ur augur	yr zephyr	eur chauffeur				
f	f fat	ff stuff	gh laugh	ph phone	ft often	lf calf					
g	g get	gg egg	gh ghost	gu guest							
h	h hot	wh who									
i	i bit	e England	o women	u busy	ui build	y hymn	ie sieve				
ī	i-e kite	y sky	ie tie	i blind	igh high	uy buy	ye rye	ei height	ai aisle	is island	
j	j jam	g gent, giant and gypsy	dge bridge	gg exaggerate	di soldier						
k	c coat	k kid	ck duck	cc acclaim	ch Christmas	lk folk	cq acquire	qu liquor			
l	l land	ll spell									
m	m me	mm summer	mb climb	lm calm	mn autumn						
n	n nut	nn bunny	kn knit	gn gnat	pn pneumonia						
ng	ng song, ring, bang and hung	ngue tongue									

Common Spellings for English Sounds

Symbol	Common Spellings of the Sound										
o	o hot	a swan	ho honest								
ō	oa boat	o-e bone	ow low	o open	oe toe	ough though	ew sew	eau beau	eo yeoman	oo brooch	
ô	a ball and walk		aw paw	or fork	au sauce	oor door	ore more	oar board	ough bought	augh taught	ar war / our four
oi	oi oil	oy boy									
ou	ou house	ow cow	ough bough								
p	p pup	pp puppy									
r	r run	rr carry	wr wrong	rh rhyme							
s	s sick	ss miss	c cent, circus and cycle		sc science	ps psychology		st listen			
sh	sh ship	ce ocean	s sure	ci special	si tension	sci conscience		ch machine	ti station		
t	t tap	tt button	th Thomas	ed tapped							
th	th thin										
TH	th then	the breathe									
u	u mug	o come	oo flood	ou double							
u̇	oo book	ou could	u full	o wolf							
ü	oo moon	ew screw	oe shoe	ue blue	ough through	u rule	ui fruit	o who	ou croup	eu maneuver	
v	v van	f of	ph Stephen								
w	w will	wh wheat	u quick	o choir							
x	x box	cks socks									
y	y yes	i opinion	j hallelujah								
yü	you you	ew few	iew view	ue cue	yu yule	eue queue	eu feud	eau beauty	ieu adieu		
z	z zero	zz buzz	s has	ss scissor	x xylophone						
zh	s measure	si division	z azure	ge garage							

How to Develop
Grapho-phonic Understanding

Grapho-phonic Understanding: 5 – 6 Reading Age

Within the first few years of formal learning these skills need to be introduced through the teacher's program to help the students to develop grapho-phonic understanding.

1. Visual Perception Leading to Discrimination: Likenesses and differences, provide matching activities that use concrete, pictorial and graphic images.

2. Kinesthetic Activities: Reading-like behaviors will develop by providing activities that;
    *   trace eye movements, as if reading a text – to follow directions – left to right, top to bottom and front to back;
    *   trace and mold shapes, letters and words.

3. Auditory Discrimination: Provide activities that highlight likenesses or differences of:
    *   initial sounds, final sounds and medial sounds (with pictures/without pictures);
    *   rhyming words.

4. Introduce all single sounds (continually revise and check): The order of investigating single sounds varies. This is one suggestion: s, t, r, c, f, h, l, a, e, i, o, u, m, n, k, j, v, p, b, g, d, (the plosive sounds p, b, g, and d can be difficult for some children) w, y, x, z, ("qu" always has a helper "u", this sound could be introduced last of all because when we make a qu sound "it feels" like the w sound). Some students may require a more thorough introduction to a particular single sound. The opportunity to investigate the sound through many class language activities, which include shared stories, daily modeled writing, rhyming activities and their own daily writing, is important.

5. Print single sounds learned. Ensure the correct formation of letters, including the starting point of letters. Some students come to school with bad habits concerning the starting points of letters. Provide encouragement to correct this problem over the year and the opportunity to revise continually. (Cursive writing, when introduced, is easier for the student to learn if all letters start correctly.)

6. Grouping of letters; for some printing lessons, investigate letter shapes according to the starting point of letters. For example:

Lower case:	c o a g d q s f	start at one o'clock
	l t k	tall letters that go from top to bottom
	i j	top to bottom
	r n m p h b	go down, back up and over
	v w	go down the hill and up
	u y	go down, around, up and down
	e x z	different from the rest
Upper case:	A B D E F H K L M N P R U V W Y	
	C G O Q S	
	I J T	
	X	
	Z	

Note: Starting points of letters may vary according to the writing style of your classroom.

Grapho-phonic Understanding: 5, 6, 7 Reading Age

1. Family words to start		he	me	she	be		so	go	no	yo-yo
		by	my	cry	dry	fly	sky	try	why	
2. Double Consonants		ss miss	ff cuff	ll hill	zz buzz	gg baggy	pp puppy	tt button rr carrot	nn funny dd daddy	mm tummy bb grubby
3. Blending: Once single sounds are recognized by the student, blend them into two-, three- or four-letter words.	**2-letter**	it	in	on	us	up	at			
	3-letter	hot	pin	run	jet	yes	Dad			
	4-letter	sand land band	jump bump pump	bent sent lent	list fist mist	best rest test	gift lift sift	miss kiss toss	buzz fizz	
4. Linking: Once the student recognizes the single sounds, link two letters that make a sound. See lists of words on pages 39 – 40.	**Initial**	tr trap	pr prim	cr crab	dr drum	fr from	br bred	gr grin	sk skip	
		st step	fl flag	sp spot	tw twig	sw swim	cl clap	bl blob	gl glad	
		pl plug	sl slip							
	Final	st best	nt bent	mp jump	ft lift	ld hold	sk desk	sp wisp		
5. Digraphs: Introduce these through daily writing, shared reading, modelled writing and other planned activities.	**Initial**	sh ship	ch chop	wh whip	th thin					
	Final	sh dish	ch rich	th moth	ck duck					
		a-e cake	o-e bone	i-e kite	ir first	ar car	oo moon	oo book	ee tree	
	ow cow	ai rain	oa coat	all ball	ing ring	ang bang	ong song	ung hung	ea leaf	
	y happy	ay tray	ow low							

6. You will need to continually revise single sounds, blending and linking skills through the classroom English program, especially through the students' own writing. The simple two-, three- and four-letter blends could form part of a basic spelling programme, for those students who can already associate the sounds of letters with the letter symbols.

7. You will notice that the students will begin incorporating single sounds and then digraphs, as they become known, in their daily writing, applying their new skills.

8. Always encourage the use of pads for all writing. The student tries spelling the word and then the teacher prints the correct spelling next to or under the student's effort. Do not interfere with the student's attempt. Praise the student for his/her effort.

9. Investigate and encourage lists of interest words as they are wanted or needed by the student and through class themes or topics. Most of these words will initially be treated as "sight" words, to "look and say".

10. Spelling Rules: Extension word endings add "s" or add "ing" to base words that do not change, e.g., desks, raining, moons, banging, coats, singing.

Remember the word examples shown are by no means exhaustive.

If a student is not ready to develop all these skills, he/she needs to be given the opportunity to gain this knowledge through re-teaching and revising the above basics.

Grapho-phonic Understanding: 6 – 7 Reading Age

At this stage of development make the student aware of the following new skills.

1. **Linking:** Revise two-letter links and extend to three letters. See pp. 39 – 40.	str string	spr sprint	thr three	scr scrap	spl splash				
2. **Digraphs:** Revise all previously taught sounds and introduce these new digraphs. See pages 21 – 38.	qu queen	ou house	oy boy	er fern	tch watch	air chair			
	ie pie	ew few	oi oil	aw paw	ur church	ear hear			
	* ice mice	*ace face	*age cage	ear pearl					
3. **Vowels:** **Short Sound**	a mat	e pet	i kit	o hop	u cut				
Long Sound	a-e mate	e-e Pete	i-e kite	o-e hope	u-e cute				
4. **Contractions:** As occur in reading and common usage.	do not don't	I am I'm	It is It's	is not isn't	cannot can't	are not aren't			
5. **Correct usage of**	is/are	has have	was were	did done	I me	a the	a an		
6. **Plurals with exceptions.**	man men	sheep sheep	deer deer	fish fish					
7. **Compound Words:** As occur in reading and common usage.	teapot playtime	rainbow sunburn	football netball	daytime popcorn	sunshine grandstand	moonbeam timetable	cowboy goldfish	raincoat inside	carport outside
8. **Word Study:** As occur in spelling lists.									
Antonyms	hot cold	like hate	you me	us them	sad happy	to from	Mom Dad	wet dry	he she
Homonyms	sail sale	made maid	pipe pipe	see sea	tee tea	fly fly	be bee	by bye buy	bow bow (and arrow)

* 'i' and 'e' and 'y' after 'g' make 'g' say 'j' (engine, cage, cabbage, gypsy)

* 'i' and 'e' and 'y' after 'c' make 'c' say 's' (circus, mice, pencil, cymbal)

9. Continually revise previously introduced single sounds, two-, three- and four-letter blends and linking skills for the consonants. See lists on pages 39 and 40.

10. Students will begin incorporating single sounds and digraphs, as they become known, into their daily writing. It is important to allow daily practice in applying these skills.

11. Always encourage the use of notepads for all writing.

12. Investigate and encourage lists of interest words and sight words as they are wanted or needed by the student. These could be formed through class topics or themes.

If a student is not ready to develop the skills outlined then he/she needs to be given the opportunity to gain this knowledge through re-teaching and revising the above basics.

13. Spelling Rules: To extend the students, introduce these skills in context as wanted or needed by the students in daily work.

- Start with adding "s", or "ing" to base words that do not change; e.g., runs, hops, sits, desks, flags, drums (simple three- and four-letter blends).

- Investigate and encourage adding "s", "ing", "er", "y", "ly" or "ed" where the base word remains the same; e.g., winds, windy, farmed, farmer, farming, farms, lifting, lifted, gladly.

- Plurals: Investigate and encourage adding "es" after "ss", "x", "ch" or "h"; e.g., foxes, dresses, washes, riches.

Grapho-phonic Understanding: 7 – 8 Reading Age

At this stage of development make the student aware of the following new skills.

1. New Digraphs: Continually revise and refer to the digraphs previously treated on pp. 7 and 8. See pp. 21 – 38 for lists of words.	ear pear	or word	ie field	ph phone	kn knit	wr wrong	mb lamb	ho honest	
	are care	dge bridge	igh high	gn gnat	st listen	lm calm	ue blue		
	ea bread	ore more	oar board	augh taught	ui build	mn autumn			
2. Contractions: As occur in reading and common usage.	we've	they've	you've	we're	they're	you're	what's	that's	won't
3. Correct usage of	was were	go goes gone	do does done	you and I	you and me	a an	a the	you're your	they're there their
4. Plurals with exceptions	woman women	tooth teeth	goose geese	child children					
5. Plurals no change	trout	sheep	deer						
6. Capitals for proper nouns	Days of week	Months of year	Names of places	Names of people					
7. Word Study as occur in spelling lists and reading text. For example:									
• **Antonyms**	last/first	before after	soft loud	end begin	awake asleep	cork uncork	throw catch	kept gave	
• **Homonyms**	two to too	sail sale	nose knows	mail male	road rode	right write	for four	flower flour	
• **Synonyms**	grass lawn	walk hike	chair seat	baby infant	raise lift	quick fast	evening night	street road	cut slice
• **Prefixes**	un- unload	re- return							
• **Suffixes**	-ing loading *waking *hopping	-ly lovely friendly	-y grassy hairy	-er harder *slipper * happier		-est softest *fittest *happiest	-ness hardness kindness	-ed banged *stopped *hurried	

*Refer to spelling rules next page

8. Investigate compound words as they occur in spelling lists and reading texts. Refer to lists on page 41; e.g., grandfather, grandmother, inside, outside, sometimes, somewhere, someone, something, somebody, himself, herself, bedroom, popcorn, nothing, afternoon, daytime, bookmark.

9. Daily dictation of a few sentences, to apply known skills, is a worthwhile activity.

10. Editing: encourage students to underline the words that need checking.

11. Begin incorporating digraphs in spelling lists as they become known. The students will begin using more known digraphs in their daily writing.

12. Encourage the use of notepads for all writing.

13. Investigate dictionary skills through alphabetical order—begin with first letter (e.g., **b**elt, **s**andbag, **w**ind) and then extend to second letter (e.g., **ba**g, **be**nt, **bo**lt, **bu**mp).

14. Investigate and encourage lists of interest words and sight words as they are wanted or needed by the students. These could be formed through class topics or themes.

If a student is not ready to develop all the skills outlined then he/she needs to be given the opportunity to gain this knowledge through re-teaching and revising the above basics.

15. Spelling Rules: Extension work for students who are ready

   • If a short vowel is followed by one consonant we need to double that consonant before we add "ing", "ed" or "y"; e.g., drum/drummed/drumming/drummer; slip/slipped/ slipping/slipper; run/runny/running; bug/buggy/bugging.

   • After "x", "ss", "sh" and "ch" we add "es".

   Add "es" to the noun to make it plural;
   e.g., box/boxes, kiss/kisses, dish/dishes, match/matches.

   Add "es" to the verb as well; e.g., wash/washes, watch/watches.

   • "y" changes to "i" and we add "es", "er", "ed", "ly", "est" or "ness"; e.g., happy, happier, happily, happiest, happiness; baby, babies, babied; puppy, puppies; easy, easier, easily, easiest; pretty, prettier, prettiest, prettily.

   • Exception to the rule – when there is a vowel before the "y" just add "s"; e.g., key/keys; donkey/donkeys; trolley/trolleys; play/plays; boy/boys; buy/buys.

   • "e" goes away when "ing" or "ed" come to stay; e.g., like/liking/liked; hope/hoped/ hoping.

   • "f" changes to "v" and we add "es"; e.g., (nouns) elf/elves; shelf/shelves; wife/wives; loaf/loaves; leaf/leaves. Note: There are exceptions; e.g., roof/roofs; hoof/hoofs.

At this stage of development make the student aware of the following new skills.

1. New Digraphs: Introduce some uncommon spellings of word families to add to the more common digraphs already taught. Continually encourage correct use of digraphs in daily work, refer to pp. 7, 8 and 9. See lists of words on pp. 21 – 38.	c circus cent cycle	aigh straight	er sergeant	tu future	u bury	ay says	eo people	i ski	
	sc science	au gauge	ough bough	ti question	ie friend	eo leopard	e equal		
		ch Christmas	oo flood	te righteous	ai said		ei receive		
	ough through	ai plaid							
2. Contractions as they occur in reading and common usage.	you're they're we're I'm	you've they've we've I've	it's that's what's	shouldn't couldn't wouldn't	won't can't isn't aren't				
3. Correct usage of collective nouns.	choir class crowd	audience team crew	mob school throng	library bouquet haul	litter herd school	shoal swarm gaggle			
4. Correct usage of masculine and feminine (where appropriate).	bride/ bridegroom	lady/ gentleman	lady/ lord	stallion/ mare	ewe/ ram	witch/ wizard/ warlock	son/ daughter		
	sister/ brother	fox/ vixen	goose/ gander	princess/ prince	grandfather/ grandmother	duck/ drake	mother/ father		
5. Correct usage of adults and progeny.	rabbit/ kitten	whale/ calf	bird/ nestling	swan/ cygnet	eagle/ eaglet	giraffe/ calf	goose/ gosling	deer/ fawn	
	sheep/ lamb	lion/ cub							
6, Word Study as occur in spelling lists and reading text. For example:									
• **Antonyms**	goodness evil	coming going	always never	written unwritten	cries laughs	loudly softly	shout whisper	bright dull	
• **Homonyms**	threw through	war wore	our hour	brake break	plane plain	right write rite	blind blind	aloud allowed	
• **Synonyms**	angry cross	over above	below beneath	open ajar	sound noise	wheat grain	lace tie	team group	
• **Prefixes**	bi- bicycle	tri- tricycle	out- outside	un- undid	over- overland	under- undertow	mid- midnight	circum- circumnavigate	
• **Suffixes**	-ful beautiful -less meatless	-hood childhood -ness darkness	-ly friendly -able portable	-y dusty -ible sensible	-let booklet -ese Japanese	-er reporter -ward toward	-or sailor	-ess princess	
7. Abbreviations, initialisms or acronyms.	USA UK NZ a.m. p.m.	Mr. Mrs. Ms. e.g. ea.	Mon. Tues. Wed. Thurs. Fri.	Sat. Sun. Jan. Feb. Mar.	Apr. Jun. Jul. Aug. Sept.	Oct. Nov. Dec. No.	St. Rd. Ave.	mm cm km kg kL	

Grapho-phonic Understanding: 8, 9, 10 Reading Age

8. Syllables: Compare words that have one, two or three syllables. Refer to some simple rules listed on page 18.

9. Root Words: Begin to introduce these through reading text. For examples of Greek and Latin origins of words see lists on page 42.

10. Investigate compound words: e.g., knockout, showroom, outdoor, indoor, bedspread, spotlight, screwdriver, horsepower, sheepdog, greenhouse, overnight, airport, girlfriend, boyfriend, campsite, grandparent, grandchild, evergreen, passport, friendship, hardship, clockwise, bookmark. See lists of words on
    page 41.

11. Revise and consolidate through applying the known skills in daily work. DAILY DICTATION of a few sentences is a worthwhile activity.

12. Editing: Encourage the student to <u>underline</u> or otherwise highlight the words that need checking.

13. Incorporate the known digraphs into class spelling lists.

14. As the students become more aware of the phonic sound spellings in words, they will use these in their daily writing. Give encouragement and praise for effort.

15. Continue to encourage the use of notepads for all writing.

16. Investigating dictionary skills through alphabetical order: Extend from first letter (e.g., dust, sailor), to second letter (e.g., outside, overland) and then third letter (e.g., present, print, proud).

17. Investigate and encourage lists of interest words and sight words as they are wanted or needed by the students. These could be formed through class topics or themes.

If a student is not ready to develop the skills outlined then he/she needs to be given the opportunity to gain this knowledge through re-teaching and revising the above basics.

18. Spelling Rules: Extension work for students who are ready
    *   If a short vowel is followed by one consonant we need to double the consonant before we add "ed", "ing" or "y"; e.g., hop/hopped, step/stepping, swim/swimming, pup/puppy.

        Words like jump and lick already have two consonants following the vowel, so just add "ing" or "ed"; e.g., jumping, licked.
    *   After "x", "ss", "sh" or "ch", we add "es" when we need to make nouns plural; e.g., watches, foxes, ashes, Christmases, masses. Do the same with verbs; e.g., splashes, wishes, fetches, boxes, misses.
    *   "y" changes to "i" when adding the suffix "es", "er", "ed", "ly", "est" or "ness"; e.g., noisy/noisily; naughty/naughtily/naughtiness/naughtier/naughtiest.

        Exception to the rule – when there is a vowel before the "y" just add the suffix "s", "er" or "ed"; e.g., valley/valleys; chimney/chimneys; enjoy/enjoyed/enjoyable/enjoyment; Thursday/Thursdays.
    *   Plurals: Change "f" to "v" and add "es"; e.g., leaf/leaves; loaf/loaves; shelf/shelves. (Remember the exceptions roof/roofs; hoof/hoofs).
    *   "e" is dropped when "ing" or "ed" is added; e.g., love/loving; hate/hated.

Grapho-phonic Understanding: 10⁺ Reading Age

At this stage of development make the student aware of the following skills.

1. **Digraphs:** Teach some of the more unusual spellings for common sounds in the English language. Revise all previously taught digraphs. See lists on pages 21 – 38. Students become aware of these sounds through the program.	et croquet	ae aesthetic	ei heifer	yr myrtle	ay quay	oe phoenix	gu guest	gue catalogue	ho honest
	ar liar	ir elixir	or doctor	ur augur	yr zephyr	dı soldier	qū liquor	cq acquire	
	pn pneumonia	E England	o women	u busy	ui build	y hymn	ie sieve	o who	o choir
	uy buy	ye rye	ei height	ai aisle	is island	ps psychology	ui fruit	i opinion	
	ough though	ew sew	eau beau	eo yeoman	oo brooch	ou soul	iew view	ou croup	j hallelujah
	ce ocean	s sure	ci special	si tension	sci conscience	ch machine	eu maneuver		
	zz buzz	ss scissors	x xylophone	eue queue	eu feud	eau beauty	ieu adieu		
	s measure	si division	z azure	ge garage					
2. **Contractions** as they occur in reading and common usage.	you're they're we're I'm	you've they've we've I've	shouldn't couldn't wouldn't won't	can't isn't aren't	should've (should have)	would've (would have)	could've (could have)		
3. **Correct usage of collective nouns.**	staff party tribe	suite flight fleet	chest stack skein	brood herd pride	company collection batch	grove clump string			
4. Masculine/Feminine (as appropriate)	nephew niece	scout guide	duke duchess	brave squaw	colt filly	buck doe			
5. **Word Study** as occur in spelling lists and reading text. For example:									
• **Antonyms**	tame wild	public private	entrance exit cheap expensive	silently noisily	midnight midday	absent present	borrow lend useful useless	afterwards beforehand changed unchanged	
• **Homonyms**	cent sent scent	worn warn	lone loan	pore pour	weigh way whey	hold holed	fourth forth		
• **Synonyms**	voyage cruise	holiday vacation	spoil ruin	eager keen	allow permit	prison jail	remain stay	stem stalk	
• **Prefixes**	semi- semicircle	up- upgrade	pro- project	mis- mistake	ex- example	anti- antidote			
• **Suffixes**	-an European	-ic telescopic	-ship partnership	-ish smallish	-al postal	-ling nestling			
6. **Abbreviations, initialisms or acronyms** Newspapers are a good source.	G.P.O. P.O. C.O.D N.B.	A SPCA SOS UFO UN	Pres. Sec. Treas. Hon.	govt. Assoc. Assn.	radar advt. Bros.	i.e. etc. fig. dia.	inc. co. p. pp.		

Grapho-phonic Understanding: 10⁺ Reading Age

7. Syllables: Compare words that have one, two or three syllables. Students need to be aware that a syllable is a part of a word usually pronounced as a unit. In dictionary work, a slash, dot or space between the syllables of the word shows syllabification. See page 18.

8. Root Words: introduce through reading material. For examples of Greek and Latin origins see list on page 42.

9. Compound Words: Newspapers are an excellent source; Examples: seafood, farmhouse, lipstick, neighborhood, ballroom, showroom, teapot, handcraft, chessboard, highway, walkway, waterway, songwriter, housework, freshwater, sunflower, dragonfly, butterfly, sandpit, worldwide, flashback, notebook, backpacker, newsletter, hardwood, softwood, heartbeat, heartache, lifestyle. (Be aware that advertisers may use non-standard compound words; e.g., lifeskills, queensize, superstore, hitouts, battlefront. Use a dictionary for reference.) For lists of compound words see page 41.

10. Daily dictation of a few sentences is worthwhile, to help revise and consolidate known sounds.

11. Students will continue to use more and more of the known digraphs in their daily writing.

12. Encourage the use of dictionaries.

13. Dictionary skills: alphabetical order extend from first letter (e.g., **c**apture, **m**idday) to second letters (e.g., **pr**ivate, **pu**blic) and then third letters (e.g., **poo**r, **por**e, **pou**r).

14. Encourage lists of interest words. Extend vocabulary according to class themes and student's interests.

If a student is not ready to develop all the skills outlined then he/she needs to be given the opportunity to gain this knowledge through re-teaching and revising the above.

15. Spelling Rules: Extension work for students who are ready

   - If a short vowel is followed by one consonant, the consonant is doubled before adding "ed", "ing", "y" or "ly"; e.g., hop/hopped; step/stepping; swim/swimming; pup/puppy; fun/funny. If you look at words like jump and lick they already have two consonants following the vowel, so just add "ing" or "ed"; e.g., jumping, licked.

   - After "x", "ss", "sh" or "ch" add "es" when making nouns plural; e.g., ashes, Christmases, masses. Do the same with verbs; e.g., splashes, wishes, fetches, boxes, misses.

   - "y" changes to "i" when adding the suffix "es", "er", "ed", "ly", "est" or "ness"; e.g., noisy/noisily; naughty/naughtily/naughtiness/naughtier/naughtiest.

   - Exception to the rule – when there is a vowel before the "y" just add the suffix "s", "er" or "ed"; e.g., valley/valleys; chimney/chimneys; enjoy/enjoyed/enjoyable/enjoyment.

   - When a word ends in "f" we need to change it to a "v" and add "es"; e.g., leaf/leaves; loaf/loaves; shelf/shelves. (Remember the exceptions; e.g., roof/roofs)

   - "e" is dropped when "ing" or "ed" is added; e.g., love/loving; hate/hated; come/coming.

Grapho-phonic Understanding: 11 – 12⁺ Reading Age

At this stage of development make the students aware of the following skills.

1. **Digraphs:** Teach some of the more unusual spellings for common sounds in the English language. Revise all previously taught digraphs. See lists on pages 21 – 38.	et croquet	ae aesthetic	ei heifer	yr myrtle	ay quay	oe phoenix	gu guest		ho honest
	ar liar	ir elixir	or doctor		ur augur	yr zephyr	di soldier	qu liquor	cq acquire
	pn pneumonia	E England	o women	u busy	ui build	y hymn	ie sieve	o who	o choir
Students become aware of these sounds through the teacher's English programme.	uy buy	ye rye	ei height	ai aisle	is island	ps psychology		ui fruit	
	ough though	ew sew	eau beau	eo yeoman	oo brooch	ou soul	iew view	ou croup	j hallelujah
	ce ocean	s sure	ci special	si tension	sci conscience		ch machine	eu maneuver	
	zz buzz	ss scissors	X xylophone			eue queue	eu feud	eau beauty	ieu adieu
	s measure	si division	z azure	ge garage					

2. **Contractions** as they occur in reading and common usage.	you're they're we're I'm	you've they've we've I've	shouldn't couldn't wouldn't won't	can't isn't aren't	should've (should have)	would've (would have)	could've (could have)		

3. **Collective Nouns –** correct usage	nest bevy troupe battery	horde board society	plague clutch galaxy	quiver	menagerie anthology constellation gathering assembly		caravan sheaf host	regiment troop battalion army platoon convoy	jury panel

4. **Occupations –** correct usage	dentist engineer florist plumber lawyer	reporter sculptor architect pilot aviator	auctioneer milliner chemist pharmacist optician		surgeon physician chiropodist veterinarian pediatrician		correspondent physiotherapist journalist chauffeur upholsterer		cartographer psychologist philatelist numismatist counselor

Grapho-phonic Understanding: 11 − 12+ Reading Age

5. Word Study as occurs in spelling lists and reading material, e.g.								
• **Antonyms**	arrange disarrange	respect disrespect frequently seldom	concrete abstract impolite polite	expand contract decrease increase	cease begin poverty wealth	majority minority disprove prove	fertile infertile insincere sincere	valuable worthless junior senior
• **Homonyms**	boarder border idol idle lone loan	isle aisle hail hale bury berry	sealing ceiling quay key seam seem	weather whether waist waste	pole poll bow beau peace piece	seen scene wheel weal practice	feint faint air heir holy wholly	bow bough allowed aloud
• **Synonyms**	elevate raise jetty wharf	umpire referee secure safe	rubbish litter buy purchase	error mistake bravery courage	fluid liquid	frozen unchanged exhibit display	ruin wreck increase expand	visitor guest exit departure
• **Prefixes**	il- illogical ir- irrelevant	inter- interschool	ac- acclaim ad- adjoin	re- reappear	sub- submarine			
• **Suffixes**	-en lighten	-tion faction	-ism realism	-ist ecologist	-ee referee	-ize computerize -ous courageous	-fy terrify -age postage	-ant deodorant -ent president
6. Abbreviations, initialisms or acronyms Newspapers are a good source.	CD-ROM RSVP Co.	TV Lat. Long. Inc. c/o	P.S. A.D. B.C. I.O.U.	fax fwd. anon. esp. www.	YMCA YWCA YMHA	UNESCO UNICEF	S.W. N.W. S.E. N.E.	

7. Syllables: Compare words that have one, two or three syllables. Students need to be aware that a syllable is a part of a word, usually pronounced as a unit. In dictionary work a slash, dot or space between the syllables of the word shows syllabification.

See list of rules on page 18.

8. Compound words: Newspapers are an excellent source; e.g., lightweight, warehouse, undergo, screenplay, software, overseas, lawmaker, graveyard, workshop, showroom, schoolroom. (Be aware that advertisers may use non-standard compound words; e.g., healthcard. Use a dictionary for reference.) See lists of words on page 41.

Grapho-phonic Understanding: 11 – 12⁺ Reading Age

9. Root Words: Introduce through reading material; e.g., refer to list on page 42.

    Greek: "phono" voice (telephone); "astro" star (astronomy); "geo" earth (geology); "hydro" water (hydroelectricity); "autos" self (autobiography); "tele" far (telephone); "aero" air (aeronautics).

    Latin: "primus" first (primitive); "aqua" water (aquatic); "annus" year (annual); "video" see (videotape); "audio" hear (audience);"civis" citizen (civilian); "mitto" send (transmit); "spiro" breathe (respiratory); "navis" ship (navigate).

10. Spelling Rules:

    • When you're not sure, look in the dictionary.

    • If a short vowel is followed by one consonant double the consonant before adding "ed", "ing" or "y"; e.g., hop/hopped; step/stepping; swim/swimming; pup/puppy; fun/funny. If you look at words like jump and lick, they already have two consonants following the vowel, so just add "ing" or "ed"; e.g., jumping, licked.

    • After "x", "ss", "sh" or "ch" add "es" to make nouns plural; e.g., ashes, Christmases, masses. Do the same with verbs e.g., splashes, wishes, fetches, boxes, misses.

    • "y" changes to "i" when adding the suffix "es", "er", "ed", "ly", "est" or "ness"; e.g., noisy/noisily; naughty/naughtily/naughtiness/naughtier/naughtiest.

    • Exception to the rule – when there is a vowel before the "y" just add the suffix "s", "er" or "ed"; e.g., valley/valleys; chimney/chimneys; enjoy/enjoyed/enjoyable/enjoyment; Thursday/Thursdays.

    • When a word ends in "f" change it to a "v" and add "es"; e.g., leaf/leaves; loaf/loaves; shelf/shelves. (Remember the exceptions; e.g., roof/roofs.)

    • "e" is dropped when "ing" or "ed" is added; e.g., love/loving; house/housing; brake/braking.

    • Words ending in "c" add a "k" before using endings which begin with "i", "e" or "y"; e.g., picnic/picnicked/picnicking/picnicker; panic/panicked/panicking/panicky.

    • Nouns that have a consonant followed by "o" need "es" to make them plural; e.g., tomato/tomatoes; potato/potatoes. BUT just add "s" if it's a musical instrument e.g., piano/pianos; banjo/banjos. Exceptions to the rule; e.g., albino/albinos. Note: Modern usage indicates a trend towards dropping the "e" in some cases; e.g., mosquito/mosquitoes/mosquitos.

    • Nouns that end with two vowels just need "s" to make them plural; e.g., radio/radios; video/videos; studio/studios; movie/movies; throe/throes; toe/toes; tie/ties.

11. Daily dictation of a few sentences will give students practice in applying known skills.

12. You could incorporate digraphs and trigraphs in class spelling lists from blue, green and red levels.

13. Encourage the use of a dictionary or thesaurus in class work. Dictionary skills: Extend to work on investigating root words and syllabification (remember a few students may still need to spell the word first).

14. Encourage lists of interest words. Extend vocabulary according to class themes, students' interests and hobbies, occupations and jargon; e.g., computer terminology.

Syllabification of Words

Here are some simple rules, which may help students understand the process of syllabification.

It is helpful to clap or tap out the sounds and, if in doubt, check in a dictionary.

1. When a word has one syllable, the word is never divided; e.g., tree, box, peace, your, love, who, wish, luck.

2. When it is a two-syllable compound word, divide between the two words; e.g., wish/bone; rain/bow; base/ball; tea/pot; pop/corn; birth/day; some/times; to/night.

3. When two or more consonants are in a word, divide the word between the first two consonants; e.g., roos/ter; lit/tle; let/ter; can/dle; wit/ches; mat/ches; cir/cus; yel/low; al/to/geth/er; dol/lars; Aus/tra/li/a.

4. When a vowel is sounded alone, it is a syllable; e.g., A/pril; par/a/chute; car/a/mel/ tel/e/scope; ban/an/a; vid/e/o.

5. When two vowels come together in a word, but are sounded separately, divide the word between the two vowels; e.g., vid/e/o; rad/i/o/ pi/an/o; ge/o/graph/y; bi/ol/o/gy.

6. **Long vowels** – when a single consonant comes between two vowels in a word, divide the word before the consonant if the first vowel is long; e.g., re/verse; mo/tor; ba/bies; la/bor; re/turn; po/ny; ti/dy; pi/rate; Ve/nus; Ju/pi/ter.

7. **Short vowels** – when a single consonant comes between two vowels in a word and the first vowel is short, divide the word after the consonant; e.g., tax/i; gar/age; dam/age; clev/er; com/ic.

8. **Prefix –** when the word has a prefix, divide the word between the prefix and the root word; e.g., un/knot; dis/please; dis/count; re/search; re/start; un/true; to/ward; un/veil.

9. **Suffix –** when the word has a suffix, divide the word between the root word and the suffix; e.g., car/ry/ing; en/joy/ment; start/ed; look/ing; play/ful; sleep/y; first/ly; haunt/ed; real/ly.

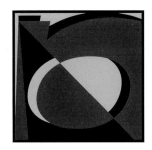

Grapho-phonic Family Word Lists

Explanation of Phonic Family Word Lists

Explanation for the Following Lists of Words

To save time, the lists of words that have been sorted into "sound" families could be used when planning for oral and written activities. (Examples of activities are on pages 44 – 55.)

The first column has the phonetic alphabet symbol for the sound.

The second and subsequent columns have lists of words with a keyword heading that relates to the common spellings for the sound. The lists of words have been color-coded to match, as far as possible, the blue, green or red age levels which were explained on pages 6 – 17.

- Check the level each student will be at – blue, green or red.

- Remember each level is following a developmental pattern.

- It is desirable for students to have an awareness or knowledge of the preceding level(s) before they are asked to tackle the next stage.

Grapho-phonic Understanding: Word Lists

Symbol

Common Spellings of the Sound

a	**a apple a hat**	**ai plaid**
	an as at am axe and ant add act amp amps attic answer ample apple addition admit admire ☺ acting action actor acid accept atom atomic Arab arid athlete athletics antler abacus absent ☺ abnormal abalone angle angler angry angrier angriest angrily annual anxiety anxious anorak annex anagram anatomy anchovy antique antelope average avocado arable allergy algebra alveoli amoeba Africa Algeria hat hatch hatbox hatpin cat catch cattle fat fatter fattest rat rattle bat batsman battle battery can canoe candle cancer ban band bantam banana fan fantasy man mango manor human pan panda panic Japan pancake pansy panel ran ranch rank drank crank bank blank plank yank tank thank sank spank shank camp camper damp damper ramp tramp trampoline mash dash rash crash sack slack stack back backlog black blackout rack racket jacket tack tackle bracket crack hack knack quack slap slash slam slant slacks nap napkin nag cab cabin cabinet cavity scab scam scram scratch swam swag sad saddle dab dabble Dad Daddy plan planned planning planner plant planet plasma flat flag flan flab flap chap chat grab gran granny grand gravel gram gradual valid vacuum zap zapped hazard happen taxi talon tattoo kangaroo raccoon	plaid plaids plaided plait plaits plaited **au laugh**

ā	**a-e** **cake**	**ai** **rain**	**ay** **tray**	**a** **baby**	**ea** **break**	**ei** **vein**	**aigh** **straight**
	face race place ace made shade age cage page cave brave bake sale tale safe brake shake snake plane hate mate plate base case chase grape bale blade behave blaze flame shape shave slave space spade stage state tame taste wage whale safety lemonade relate translate indicate illuminate anticipate pavement bravery airplane	train tail pail main pain maid mail sail laid aim bait fail hail wait stain chain afraid unafraid grain mainly painting painted unchain aimless failure faint paid ailment brain plain raise railway remain trail waist Spain daily sailor waif gait braise airmail bailiff braille maintain	say clay may pray pay slay relay bay hay ray day today yesterday birthday holiday Sunday Monday Tuesday Wednesday Thursday Friday Saturday fray railway display essay byway airway betray crayon defray hooray heyday layout mayhem runway	apron April lady ladies baby babies babied paper papers able cable table stable alien pastry laser radio Australia taste waste lazy hazy crazy potato native nature famous strange stranger strangest strangely danger endanger dangerous association evaporating patience patients grazier patriarch pastries palatial	great greater greatest greatness break breaks steak steaks **ey** **they** they prey hey obey obeying survey surveying surveyed surveyor	veins veil veils veiling rein reins skein skeins reindeer **eigh** **weigh** eight eighteen eighty sleigh neigh neighing neighbor neighborhood weigh weight heavyweight lightweight freight freighting freighted	straight straightaway straighten **et** **croquet** croquet crochet crocheted crocheting bouquet bouquets **au** **gauge** gauge gauged gauging gaugeable gauger

The Complete Phonic Handbook

21

Grapho-phonic Understanding: Word Lists

Symbol   **Common Spellings of the Sound**

ā

are
care

care careful careless caring cared carefully carefulness carelessness carefree uncaring caretaker bare barely barest bareback barehanded barefooted dare daring dared daredevil fare fares faring glare glaring hare hares mare mares nightmare square squares squarely pare pared paring prepare prepared preparing parent parentage rare rarely rarer rarest rarity rarify stare staring stared share sharing shared shareholder shareholding scare scared scaring scarecrow scaredy cat scarce scarcely snare snaring snared spare spared sparing sparingly ware aware warehouse warehousing silverware tinware glassware software hardware

air
chair

air airbag aircraft aircrew airdrop airflow airport airmail airman airway chair chairs chairman chairwoman chairperson chairlift wheelchair dairy dairies dairying dairymaid fair fairground fairs fairway fairy fairies fairyland fairground fairway fairylike fairytale hair hairs hairy hairdo hairbrush hairdresser hairiness hairdressing hairless lair lairs laird lairdship pair pairs paired pairing repair repaired repairing stair stairs stairway staircase stairwell

ear
pear

bear bears bearing beared bearer bearhug bearskin pear pears wear wears wearer wearing wearable wear out wear off wear down

ere
where

where whereabouts whereas whereby wherefore whereupon wherever whereupon everywhere anywhere somewhere nowhere there thereabouts thereby thereafter therefore therein thereon thereupon

eir
their

their theirs

ayer
prayer

prayer prayers

ä

ar
car

car cars carport carpet carpets cargo jar jars jarring jarred arm arms armed arming army armies bar bark barking barked barbecue barbecued barbecuing barber barley barn barometer harsh dark darker darkness darn darning harm charm charming harmless harming harmful farm farms farming farmed farmer farmhouse farmhand farmland farmyard art artist artists far farther farthest mark marking unmarked marker star stars starring starred starch starchy starched stardust starfish starling starlight start starting started startle starve starving starved sharp sharpen sharpness sharply shark sharks smart mark market marble March marvellous parcel parcels park parks parka parked parking parkland parkway part parted parting party parties partying partly participate participant particle particular partial depart departure parch parched pardon parliament parliamentarian parliamentary parquetry parsley parsnip target garland large larger largely

ear
heart

heart hearts heartbeat heartache heartburn heartless heartfelt heartland heartily heartbroken heartworm

er
sergeant

sergeant sergeants

Grapho-phonic Understanding: Word Lists

Symbol	Common Spellings of the Sound

<table>
<tr><td rowspan="2">b</td><td colspan="1">b
bat</td><td>bb
rabbit</td></tr>
<tr><td>bat bats batting batted batter but butter buttered buttering bet bets better bettered bettering bit bitter bitterly bitters bottom bottle bonny bonfire ban banner banners band bands bend bending bent beneath bin bins bind binds binding bonbon bond bonding bonded bun buns bunny bunch bunches bunched bunching bad badly bed beds bedroom bedrooms bedding bedside bid bids bidding body bodies bodied bodily bone bones boned bony bud buds budding budded buddy buddies box boxed boxing boxes bag bags bagged bagging beg begs beggar beggars begging begged big bigger biggest bog boggle bogged bogging bug bugs bugged bugging bus bused busing buses batch butch butcher botch botched beauty beautiful beautifully butterfly butterflies bottle bottled bottles beach beat beam beast beads beak bean beard beaver bee beef beetle beetles be become became began begin begun behind because beneath before below beware believe belong behave beside by bye buy ball balloon ballroom bike bikes bird birds birdcage birdseed book boom buzz bump bumped bumping bake baker baker back backed backing biology</td><td>rabbit rabbits abbey abbot cabbie robber robbers robbed robbing robbery rubber rubbing rubbed bubble bubbles bubbled bubbly cabbage cabbages ribbon ribbons ribboned ribboning wobble wobbling wobbly babble babbling bobbed bobbin bobble cobber cobblestones dabble fobbed gabble gibbon gobble hobble pebble pebbly squabble squabbled squabbling rabble mobbed mobbing nabbed nabbing scabby shabby stubby stubbed tabbed webbed webbing clubbed clubbing dabbing drabble fibbing grabbed grubbed cobbler hobbler knobby lobbing Sabbath stubble blabbing crabbing dribbler</td></tr>
</table>

<table>
<tr><td rowspan="2">ch</td><td>ch
rich child</td><td>tch
watch</td><td>tu
future</td><td>ti
question</td></tr>
<tr><td>chop chops chopping chopped chat chats chatting chatted chick chicks chicken cheese cheeses chip chips chipping chipped check checked checking checks child children change changed unchanged changes changing chance chances chanced choke choked choking chain chains chaining chained cheek cheeks cheeky cheat cheating cheated chew chewed chewing chuck chucking cheer cheering church churches chose chosen chase chased chasing chases inch inches pinch branch branches bunch bunched bunches lunch lunches torch torches torched touch touched touching untouched bench benches peach peaches beach beaches teach teaches teacher teachers teaching search searched searching searches unsearchable</td><td>watch watches watching watched match matches matched matching hatch hatches hatched hatching latch latches latched latching patch patched patching patches catch catches catching fetch fetched fetching fetches sketch sketched sketching sketches witch witches ditch ditches ditched ditching hitch hitching pitch pitched pitches pitching stitch stitched stitches stitching botch butcher butchers butchered kitchen kitchens itch itchy itching itches itched</td><td>future adventure nature capture picture fracture manufacture creature feature structure puncture denture moisture pasture posture stature</td><td>question
te
righteous
righteous</td></tr>
</table>

Grapho-phonic Understanding: Word Lists

Symbol

Common Spellings of the Sound

d	d dad	dd add	ed filled
	dad dads daddy did didn't do don't does doesn't dab dabbing dub dubbing duck ducking ducks deck decks decking dock docking docked die dies died dying dead deadly doe day days daytime dagger dog dogs dig digs digging dug daffodil different differently definite definitely definition daily dam dams damp dammed damming damping demonstrate demonstrating diminish dominate dance danced dancing dances dancer donate donation donations donated door doors doorway dot dotted dotting double dove down downward downwards downstairs doze dozes dozen deposit deposited depositing desk desks determine determined devil dew dewdrops dappled dare daring dared destroy destroyed daughter dawdle daze dazzle dazzling direct direction directly distant distantly distance distances	add adds adding added addition addict addicted ladder ladders adder caddy daddy sadden sadder saddle saddled saddling saddlery wedding wedded address addresses addressed sudden suddenly giddy giddiness muddy buddy redder reddest reddish bladder doddery faddish griddle maddest madder maddening middle puddle puddles fiddle fiddler fiddling riddle riddles riddled twiddle twiddling twiddled cuddle cuddled cuddling cuddles pudding huddle huddling huddled huddles muddle muddling meddle meddling meddled odd oddment oddly peddling plodded plodder fodder prodded prodding shredder shredded shredding shudder shuddering shuddered skidded skidding studded swaddle swaddling swaddled thudded twaddle wadding waddle waddling befuddled	filled billed chilled grilled frilled grilled hilled killed milled stilled willed farmed calmed dammed armed harmed alarmed palmed tamed lined dined fined mined pined signed timed wined waved behaved craved starved starred charred rained nailed strained sprained drained framed blamed maimed stained trained scanned planned manned fanned zoomed doomed bloomed boomed loomed entombed combed climbed reigned feigned signalled wriggled triggered whistled manufactured fractured

e	e let	ea bread	a many	ie friend	eo leopard
	let letter very lettering letters bet better bettered met metal wet wetter get getting jet jetting jetted kept net netball netballer pet felt carpet set setting settle unsettle yet fetch never seven bed bedding bedroom bedspread else engine elephant beg begging beggar bell bells best bellow bellows fresh freshly pen pencil egg eggs enjoy petrol help helpmate yell yellow slept crept depth cleft left send spend held mend bend lend sent cent scent spent misspent lent mention bent tent dentist elf shelf self enter entrance centre central belt deck ever	bread breads read ready spread spreads spreading tread treading dead deadly feather feathers feathering leather leathers leathering weather weathering weathered stead homestead heavy heavier heaviest heavily head headache headband headboard headdress header headgear heading headlamp headlight headland headlong headmaster headpiece headphone headway headrest headstand headstrong thread threads threading breakfast breakfasts pleasant pleasantly pheasant pheasants breath weapon weapons weaponry leaded unleaded lead deaf deafening	many any anymore anyone anything anybody anyway anyhow anywhere **ei** **heifer** heifer heifers leisure leisurely leisurewear leisured	friend friends friendly friendlier friendliest unfriendly friendship friendliness friendless befriend befriended **ai** **said** said **ay** **says** says	leopard leopardess **u** **bury** bury buries buried burial burials burying **ae** **aesthetic** aesthetic aesthetics anaesthetic anaesthetics anaesthesia anaesthetize anaesthetists anaesthesiologist (US)

Grapho-phonic Understanding: Word Lists

Symbol			Common Spellings of the Sound			

ē	ee bee	ea leaf	y happy	ey key	i ski and machine	e equal	ie chief
	bee beet	leaf leaves	happy happily	key keys keyed	ski skis skied	equal equally	chief chiefs
	beetroot	beak beaks	unhappy any	keyboard	taxi taxis	equalize	chiefly brief
	between sleep	beads beaded	many baby body	donkey	spaghetti	equidistant me	briefs briefly
	asleep cheek	bean beans	anybody easy	donkeys	confetti	he we be she	debrief thief
	cheeks cheeky	beanstalk	lady party ready	monkey	piano pizza	e-mail ego	thieves
	creek creeks	cheap cheaper	very pretty	monkeys	radio	recipe emu	thieving grief
	cheese cheeses	cheapest clean	funny carry	money honey	orientation	even evening	grieves grieved
	cheer cheered	cleaner	carrying puppy	journey	Australia	evil video	relief relieves
	cheering	cleanest	windy cheeky	journeys valley	Australian	videotape	piece pieces
	green	cream creamy	twenty thirty	valleys volley	unique	secret secretly	pieced piecing
	evergreen	icecream deal	forty fifty sixty	volleyball	uniquely	senior stereo	belief believe
	greenhouse	dealer dream	seventy eighty	jockey trolley	potpourri	stereotype	believes
	free freedom	dreamily	ninety dirty	turkey parsley		theater legal	believed
	freely	dreaming eager	family nobody	jersey chimney	machine	legion region	believer
	guarantee keen	eagles east	busy city pony	chimneys alley	machines	retail return	retrieve
	keenly knee	Easter eastern	tiny angry	alleys odyssey	machinery	reverse reveal	retriever
	meet meeting	easterly easy	hungry plenty	honeybee	machining	reception	retrieved
	thirteen	easier easily	every everyone		routine	decide detour	retrieving
	fourteen	uneasy gleam	merry hurry	ei receive	routines	female femur	movie movies
	fifteen sixteen	heat heated	hurrying sorry	receives	routinely	frequent	pastries diesel
	seventeen	heats ideal lead	jelly silly sunny	receiver	police policing	frequency	shriek shrieking
	eighteen	leader leading	lucky tummy	receiving	policed	facsimile	shrieked shield
	nineteen seen	least mean	naughty	received	policeman	behind before	shielding
	sheet sheep	meaning	geography	deceive	policewoman	below beyond	shielded
	spreadsheet	meaningful	history beauty	deceives	magazine	began begin	shields priest
	sheepskin	meat neat	company	deceived	tangerine	begun because	priests field
	screenplay	neatly neatest	January February	deceiver	tambourine	believe	fielding fielded
	sneeze steel	peace plea	library noisy	deceiving	guillotine	unbelievable	fields wield
	sneezed	please real	thirsty worry	conceive	limousine elite	concrete ether	wielding
	sneezing steep	really unreal	galaxy country	conceives	ravine marine	ethos	wielded frieze
	steeper	realism reason	remedy delivery	conceiving	morphine	equilateral	friezes aggrieve
	steepest	reasoning reach	recovery	conceived	cuisine	excretion	disbelieve spiel
	steeply street	reaches	property quality	conceiver	gasoline	ecology	glockenspiel
	streets speed	reaching	balmy tragedy	inconceivable	nectarine	ecosystem gene	afield airfield
	speeding	reached scream	rhapsody	perceive	figurine	genus genius	infield outfield
	sightseeing	screaming	jeopardy subsidy	perceives	quarantine	geology	minefield
	three tree	screamed	melody custody	perceived	submarine	geologist	battlefield
	peel peeled	season seasons	comedy parody	perceiving	sardine	geometry	
	peeling	speak speaker	clergy prodigy	unperceived		geography	eo people
	proceed	speaking steam	eulogy allergy	either neither	oe phoenix	Indonesia	people peoples
	proceeding	steaming	ecstasy pleurisy	seize seizing	phoenix	media meter	peopled
	queen	steamed stream	embassy cruelty	seized seizes		millimeter	
	windscreen	teach teaches	dignity cavity	caffeine		centimeter	
	wheel wheels	teacher	gravity floppy			kilometer	
		teaching tease	wallaby enemy			penal sequins	
		teases teased	Italy Germany			sequel vehicle	
		teasing beach	Tuscany duty				
		beaches weak	duty-free luxury				
		weaker weakest	laundry felony				
			tyranny dairy				
			fairy pregnancy				
			infancy				
			pharmacy				

Grapho-phonic Understanding: Word Lists

Symbol	Common Spellings of the Sound			

ėr	ir **first**	er **fern**	ur **church**	ear **pearl**	or **word**
	first firstly **bird** birds	fern ferns herb yesterday herbs	church churches	pearl pearls	**word** words
	birth birthday birthdays	average serve service conserve	nurse nursing	pearling pearler	wordy worded
	chirp chirps chirping	conservation reserve reservation	nursed purse	**earn** earning	**work** worker
	dirt dirty dirtier dirtiest	reverse reversing every	purses **fur** furry	earned **earth**	worked workers
	dirtily **fir** firm firmly	everything everyone everywhere	**furs turn** return	earthed **earthly**	working
	firmer firmest **confirm**	federal govern government	returned turtle	earthquake **heard**	workplace
	girl girls **girth mirth sir**	person personnel personality	returning turtles	unheard **learn**	homework
	stir shirt shirts **skirt**	interstate western eastern	churn churns **burn**	learned learning	framework
	skirts skirted skirting	northern southern overall	**burnt burns burgle**	search searches	unworkable
	circus circuses third	overalls overtime overnight	suburb burglar	searched searching	worse worst
	thirds thirdly thirteen	property interest interesting	burgundy furnish	searchingly	worth worthy
	thirteenth thirty	interested uninteresting general	furnishes	research	worthwhile
	thirtieth thirst thirsty	generally liberty waterfront	furnished	researched	unworthy **effort**
	thirstier thirstiest	expert modern certainly	furnishing	researching	effortless motor
	virtues virtual virtually	understand understood operate	furniture **further**	**yr**	motors motored
	circle circles circled	operation wonderful bravery	figures futures	**myrtle**	motoring
	circling semicircle	interact supersonic different	injured natural	myrtle	motorist
	circular circumference	exercise artery emergency	purple **purpose**	myrrh	motorists author
	circumstance	gallery robbery lottery lotteries	Saturday Thursday	**our**	authorization
	circumnavigate	insert certain insertion perfume	surprise surprises	**journey**	investors minors
	aur	university Germany permanent		journey journal	sailors decorate
	restaurant	mineral minerals characteristics		journalist	decorated
		commercial		journalism adjourn	visitors network
					artwork

∂r	er **mother**	ar **liar**	or **doctor**	ur **augur**
	mother other another brother bother	liar collar dollar	doctor liquor sector investor	augur femur recur
	after father rather **sister** letter better	scholar cedar	administrator director motor	concur occur demur
	butter dinner grandfather grandmother	cheddar nectar	author minor sailor error visitor	murmur
	under paper newspaper summer winter	cellar stellar	tailor surveyor razor anchor	**ure**
	number computer weather deliver	briar friar vicar	cantor pastor castor hector	**pleasure**
	water river worker offer **flycatcher**	pillar molar	protector elector inspector	pleasure measure
	September October November	polar solar altar	collector reflector selector	treasure leisure
	December damper docker ever never	Gibraltar mortar	objector injector censor sensor	disfigure
	forever clever owner **answer lawyer**	lunar sublunar	tormentor inventor confessor	transfigure injure
	cancer power flower buyer over cover	calendar	professor compressor oppressor	fissure
	discover Easter wonder wander gather	binocular	successor possessor debtor	**yr**
	together proper danger finger master	**ir**	abettor prior survivor visor	**zephyr**
	quarter silver ladder matter robber	**elixir**	incisor exhibitor predictor	zephyr martyr
	rubber supper enter slipper soldier	elixir choir	constrictor evictor donor stupor	**eur**
	weather whether butcher baker teacher		juror conductor instructor	chauffeur
	maker grocer miner hammer **helicopter**		extractor emperor bachelor	connoisseur
	daughter eager either leather plaster		**our**	amateur Pasteur
	powder ruler saucer spider thunder		**hour**	
	timber retailer peacemaker stranger		hour flour	
	ranger scanner grasshopper improper			
	dispatche			

Grapho-phonic Understanding: Word Lists

| Symbol | | Common Spellings of the Sound | | |

f	ff **stuff**	f **fat**	ph **phone**	gh **laugh**
	stuff off offer huff buff	fat fib fig fix fin fit fun felt	phone phoning phoned	laugh laughing laughed
	bluff bluffed gruff puff	funny fir fur fill full	telephone nephew nephews	laughable cough coughing
	stuff stuffed staff staffing	fall fell foal five fire fine	orphan orphans	coughed rough roughly
	stiff stiffen gaff gaffed cuff	fern fuss feet foam farm	megaphone xylophone	tough toughened toughly
	cuffs scuff scuffing scuffed	foot football fish fizz fuzz	microphone saxophone	tougher toughest trough
	sniff sniffle sniffling scoff	food fool form fuse furl foil	dictaphone graph	troughs enough draught
	scoffs scoffing duffle	fold face fair fairy fast	autograph photograph	draughts draughty slough
	muffin raffle buffoon	father fear fence find fight	telegraph lithograph	sloughs
	shuffle suffer suffice	fixture feud folk for four	monograph phonograph	
	handcuff coffin puffer	fore forgive found fiddle	cenotaph phantom phonics	**ft** **often**
	paraffin offend offense	first fatal fiber film fitness	symphonic euphony	often soften
	office officer affect	fault fountain furniture	phosphorous pharmacy	
	affection affected effect	family fetch few field	physics physical physician	**lf** **calf**
	effects effected efficient	fifteen fifth fifty finish fort	physique Philippines	calf half
	sufficient giraffe suffix	follow forest forget	typhoon elephant dolphin	
	chauffeur chauffeuring	fortnight forty fourteen	morphine apostrophe	
		faint feint famous fancy	triumphant sphere	
		fare fasten February Friday	hemisphere stratosphere	
		fellow figure forgotten	ionosphere	
		fortune fought fourth deaf		
		elf self shelf myself himself		
		herself yourself itself rifle		
		trifle stifle wife life knife		
		carafe Fahrenheit		

g	g **get**	gg **egg**	gh **ghost**	gu **guest**
	get getting got go going gone goes	egg eggs bigger beggar	ghost ghosts ghostly	guest guests guess
	goose geese gate girl goat gold	begging begged ragged	ghosting ghoul ghoulish	guessing guessed guide
	gap gas gay gum gun gain gale	digging rigged rigging	ghastly gherkin ghetto(s)	guided guiding
	game gang gasp gift gifted gave	bagging bagged bogged	**gue** **dialogue**	guidepost guidebook
	gaze give given golf good gown	bogging bugged bugging		guideline guidance
	gulf gull gulp gush gust gaunt	digging foggy soggy	dialogue monologue	guard guards guarding
	gawk gauze gallon gallop garden	flagged flagging gagged	synagogue vague vogue	guarded guardian
	galore gambol gamble gander	gagging bragging	league fatigue plague	guardian angel guild
	garage gargle garlic garter gather	bragged stagger	intrigue colleague	guildhall guilt guilty
	gassed goodbye golfer golden god	staggering struggle		guinea guinea pig
	gospel gossip govern gallant	struggled struggling		guinea fowl guitar
	gallery gallows gangway garbage	juggle juggling juggled		guitarist guise disguise
	garland garment garnish gaseous	hugging hugged plugged		guarantee guaranteed
	gastric gathers gazelle gingham	plugging rugged drugged		guarantor guerilla
	girlish goddess goggles gondola	drugging dragged		guillotine
	gorilla gosling gourmet gunboat	dragging dagger daggers		
	galactic gamebird gangland	tagged tagging wagging		
	gangster gangrene gardener	wagged		
	gaslight gasoline gauntlet godchild			
	goldfish goldfield goldmine			
	goldfinch goodwill gorgeous			
	governor government			

Grapho-phonic Understanding: Word Lists

Symbol   **Common Spellings of the Sound**

h	h	wh
	hot	**who**
	hot hat hit hut heat hid hop hip happy huff hug hog him ham hem hum hand head has had have how her hang held hunt help hall hike hook home hate harm hope horn hubcap horse house hair hear here half high himself holiday herself hurry happen heard heart hurrah honey hospital hind huge howl hurl husk hundred hungry hail herd hopped hoped hotel hammer handle health heavy heavier heaviest hedge helicopter hiding hidden history husband habit helmet heyday hockey hoist hooray healthy haircut hammock hamster harmony harmful harbor hateful halve hairy horde haven hound haunt haughty hearsay heroine hero hexagon highway horror hazard handle homonym hormone hostage hostess hurried hydrant hallmark handbook handcuff handicap handmade handsome handyman hangover hardware harmless hatchery haunting haystack headache headband heaven hedge heredity heritage hijacker human humidity humour humorous humpback hygiene hygienic hypnosis hysteric hymn heifer hybrid	**who** whose whom whole wholehearted wholemeal wholesale wholesome wholewheat wholly whoever whomever whomsoever

i	i	y	u
	bit	**hymn**	**busy**
	bit hit fit hit lit mitt nit pit sit wit him dim rim win bin din fin kin pin tin bib fib nib bid did hid kid lid rid sniff stiff whiff big dig fig jig pig rig rigger wig with fifth gift lift rift sift shift middle video kick brick chick flick lick pick sick stick wick bill chill still miss fill gill hill drill kill nil pill will spill chip dip six drip flip grip hip clip lip rip ripple whip silly sister fist kiss list mist quiz wrist sixty sixteen sixth pixie risk wind window quick quickly rabbit river animal April bridge history chicken comic cricket different family fifty fifteen insect instead invite kitchen listen magic minutes music office pencil picnic which witch picture fixture distance mixture prince princess slippers terrible until artist beginning cabin capital Christmas ditch divide division electric figure history important interest knit midnight pillow porridge prison public prisoner ribbons signal silken timber whistle written	hymn hymns gym gymnastics pyjamas pyramid mystery mysticism myth myths mythological symbol symbolic cymbal cymbals sympathy sympathetic gypsy gypsies Egypt Egyptian syringe syringes cyst cysts tryst trysts crypt cryptic lymph nymph nymphs glycerine analyst catalyst cataclysm hypocrite hypnosis hypnotism chlorophyll synonym antonym homonym pseudonym **o** **women** women womenfolk **E** **England** England English	**busy** busy busier busiest busily business minute minutes **ui** **build** build builder rebuild building builds built rebuilt guild guilds guilt guilty guillotine guillotines guillotined guinea guineas guinea fowl **ie** **sieve** sieve sieved sieves handkerchief mischief

Grapho-phonic Understanding: Word Lists

Symbol

Common Spellings of the Sound

ĩ	i–e kite	y sky	i blind	igh high	ei height
	kite bite dive drive fire hire	sky by my	blind mind find hind kind	high fight	height heights
	alive line fine mine nine tide	dry cry try	rind grind bind behind	light might	heightening either
	side aside hide wide time quite	fry fly ply	unkind unwind mild wild	nighty plight	neither Fahrenheit
	rite site pride smile white while	sly spry July	child climb liar briar friar	right sight tight	edelweiss sleight
	chime wireless online wise wife	decry outcry	prior grandchild godchild	bight knight	kaleidoscope
	clockwise website hotline grime	rely apply	mastermind trial triad	flight fighter	**is**
	prime lifetime polite excite	butterfly	triangle triangular tricycle	fighting	**island**
	mobile satellite worldwide	dragonfly	tripod Triassic triennial via	delight	island islands isle
	scribe advice describe device	multiply	vial viable vibrant dial redial	twilight	isles islet
	prescribe subscribe decide guide	reply apply	giant quiet diet client riot	skylight	**ye**
	outside decide retire seaside	reapply type	cider wider spider glider Bible	moonlight	**rye**
	housewife knife strike reptile	retype	tribal arrival virus alibi	sunlight	rye bye goodbye
	compile exile twine shrine	typecast	biceps bionic biopsy biplane	floodlight	dye dyes dyeing
	overtime perspire transpire	occupy	bipod bicycle bilateral	daylight	dyed lye eye eyes
	stalagmite stalactite appetite	qualify	biology biannual biennial	birthright	eyed eyeing
	subside bedside topside	magnify	microphone	playwright	**uy**
	crocodile lifelike dislike	terrify	**sign**	copyright	**buy**
	countryside offside riverside	horrify	sigh signs signed align	fortnight	buy buys buying
	mountainside nationwide	classify	aligned malign maligned	oversight	buyer guy guyed
	juvenile infantile turnstile	satisfy	benign assign assigned	hindsight	guying
	pantomime maritime canine	pigsty	assignment design designed	**ie**	**ai**
	feline windpipe paradise termite	cyanide	designing resign resigned	**tie**	**aisle**
	parasite baptize capsize survive	rhyme	resigning consign realign	tie lie die died	aisle aisles
	porcupine calamine turpentine	thyme lyre	countersign undersign	pie pies untie	Thailand Thai
	alpine airline	awry cycle	undersigned	underlie magpie	
	provide	hyphen		necktie	

j	j jam	g gentle, giant and gypsy	dge bridge
	jam jab jag jet jig job jug jar joy jaw	rage cage page stage cages pages stages luggage cabbage	bridge ridge
	jazz jell jest jilt jinx jolt jump junk	gentle gent gel gem gene germ genie genre genus gender	midge edge
	just jade jail jeans jeep jelly jive join	genius gentle gently gentry gerbil German gelatine general	hedge ledge
	joke July June jury Japan jaunt jetty	genuine geology gesture germinate gemstone generate	fledge pledge
	jewel joint joist jolly judge juice juicy	generous genetics genocide geometry geometric geography	dredge wedge
	juror jackal jacket jaguar jailer jalopy	geranium pigeon baggage damage garage package leakage	budge nudge
	jammed jangle jargon jasper jersey	message sausage postage language voyage average heritage	fudge trudge
	jester jetsam jiggle Jew jigsaw jockey	oxygen nitrogen negligent negligence digestion tragedy	smudge
	jostle jovial joyful jugful juggle	imagery congeal allege beverage anchorage patronage	grudge
	jumble jumper jungle junior jabbed	pilgrimage carnage dosage vegetable vegetate village danger	sludge
	jackass jackpot janitor January	dangerous charge splurge scourge urge merge purge submerge	**gg**
	jasmine javelin jawbone jaywalk	emerge emergency **giant** magic gin gist ginger giraffe	**exaggerate**
	jazzman jealous jewelery jugular	giantism gigantic gingerly magician magical magically engine	exaggerate
	jonquil journal journey joyride	engineer energetic gingerbread giblets regiment region	exaggeration
	jukebox Jupiter justice justify	regional register registrar registration legend legendary	suggest
	jeopardy jettison jeweler jodhpurs	legible legislate legislative legitimate magistrate **gypsy** gym	suggestion
	joyfully joystick jumpsuit junction	gymnast gymnastics gymkhana energy	
	juvenile	**di** **soldier**	
		soldier soldiers soldiered soldiering	

Grapho-phonic Understanding: Word Lists

Symbol   **Common Spellings of the Sound**

k	c **coat**	k **kid**	ck **duck**	ch **Christmas**	lk **folk**	cq **acquire**
	cat cap cab can cot	kid kill king kind	duck back kick	Christmas Christ	folk folks folktale	acquire
	cob come came cost	key kept kick kite	deck stick stuck	Christian	folklore kinfolk	acquired
	cow camp cage care	kitten kiss kennel	black block sock	chemical chemist	townsfolk yolk	acquiring
	carry catch cave coal	keen kettle keel	socks track trick	chemistry chord	yolked yolkless	acquires
	corn case cold cork	keep kitchen	stack lick lock	choral choir	**cc** **acclaim**	acquaint
	cargo comic corner	kangaroo koala	luck suck truck	chorus chronic	acclaim accurate	acquainted
	coast count could	kisses kissed	quick brick crack	chronicle	accommodate	acquaintance
	cover can't copy	kidded kiosk	ticket cricket	chronological	accommodation	acquit
	carrot cattle captain	kidding kindness	packet pocket	choreography	accordion	acquittal
	carpet castle caught	kaleidoscope	rocket flock	chlorine	account	**qu** **liquor**
	color country cousin	kapok kayak	knock clock	chromosome	accounting	liquor
	calf cabbage cabin	keepsake kelp	o'clock chicken	chlorophyll	accountant	liquorice
	calm camel candle	keratin kerosene	struck checked	chrysalis	accumulate	liquid
	capital capture	kerb kernel	checking trickery	chrysanthemum	accuse accustom	
	careful cause collar	kestrel ketch	cricketer	technique		
	comb common	kidnap kidney	pocketing unlock	technical		
	company correct	kiln kilogram	unblock unlucky	technician		
	couple coming cough	kiloliter kilometer	unluckily stock	technology		
	carriage carried	kilowatt kudu	stockings	technicolor		
	carrying catcher		sunblock	technological		
	complain calculate					
	constant					

l	l **land**	ll **spell**
	land lad lag lap lass led leg less let lid lift lip list lob	spell spelling doll ball call fall gall hall mall tall wall
	log lot lug lump like lick left luck love loud lone loss	yell sell cell hell dell fell tell well will ill bill sill still
	loam loft load lack lock lamp little live lame lizard limb	chill dill fill gill grill hill kill mill pill bull cull dull full
	lamb lick law lard lawn lay lazy loud last lie life letter	gull hull lull pull bulldog bullfrog stall jelly holly jolly
	leaf leaves leave lady ladies lace ladder luggage laid	shell smell dwell swell collie poll roll droll scroll troll
	large loom laugh lead learn learned least lovely lucky	stroll toll payroll yellow mellow volley bully fully pulley
	luckily lying lightning lash lashes lasses latch lime	hello skill spill drill frill grill shrill quill swill twill
	latched listening listened lint listener lacquer lactose	shilling thrill thrilling trolley folly belle roller stroller
	language lantern lanolin lapse larva lava larynx lather	marshmallow recalled baseball basketball football
	lathe latitude longitude lattice latter launch laughter	softball dally rally tally refill downhill uphill treadmill
	laundry lavender lavish league leakage lecture leech	windmill standstill waterfall blackball pinball snowball
	leach lease leasing leased legal legend length lumber	windfall rainfall snowfall nightfall callow shallow fallow
	lugger lunar lung luncheon legislate legislator	mallow sallow tallow willow chenille halloween bluebell
	legislation legitimate legume lenient lens lounge louver	cowbell misspell farewell parallel oversell cockleshell
	leopard leotard leprosy lettuce level levy liable liberal	unwilling billion million trillion rebelled repelled
	license lichen lieutenant ligament lilac limited linear	compelled propelled expelled dispelled excelled
	liquidate literacy literature lobster local locality loch	excellent alley hillside ballet ballot swallow swallowed
	locate locomotion locomotive lodge locust logic logical	swallowing gorilla guerilla collision atoll controlled
	location loneliness loin luminous lymph lyric lyre	uncontrolled controller patroller bulldozer bulldozing
		crystalline chlorophyll pollute pollution polluted illusion
		balloonist

Grapho-phonic Understanding: Word Lists

Symbol   **Common Spellings of the Sound**

m	**m** **me**	**mm** **summer**	**mb** **climb**
	me met mitt mop map mad man mark mat matter meet meal meat must mast mask my myself most mist mow mower made maid make mail male many mate mice mile more moth mother morning might main marker magic master merry middle mitten minutes money monkey month mouth movie mountain mouse move moon metal medal mushroom music magical manage marble March Monday market marry match matches melt message midnight miner moment mince mind motor movement mutton macaroon mace machine macrame magazine magenta magistrate magnet magnetic magnificent magnitude mayhem maintain maintenance major mayor material malignant malign mammoth management mangrove manger manufacture marathon manuscript marine margin marketing maritime marmalade marriage marshmallow marsupial marrow masculine mathematics maximum minimum miniature ministry mirror maze measure measurement mechanical medicine medium memoir memorial memory myth mythology meningitis Mercury meridian mesmerize millimeter meter murmur muscle mussel molluscs metamorphosis metropolitan microbe microscope military million millipede miscellaneous mischief mischievous misunderstood modern modernize monument motorist mountainous mourn multiply multiplication multiples mural mustard	summer simmer shimmering slimmer slimming shimmer shimmering shimmered swimmer swimming dummy mummy drummed drummer drumming hammer hammering hammered grammar jammed slammer slammed slamming crammed brimmed trimmed slimmed sledgehammer windjammer dammed damming rammed ramming crammed cramming stammered common dimmed skimmed rimmed command commander comment comments commence commenced commencing communist scrimmage gimmick trimmest dimmest slimmest primmest mummify	climb climbed climbing limb limbs lamb lambs lambing comb combing crumb crumbs crumbed crumbing crumby numb numbing numbed thumb thumbs thumbing plumber plumbing dumb dumber bomb bomber bombed bombing **lm** **calm** calm calming becalmed becalm palm palms psalm psalms qualm qualms **mn** **autumn** autumn column columnist damn damned damning hymn hymns

n	**n** **nut**	**nn** **bunny**	**kn** **knit**	**gn** **gnat**
	nut nag name nap net neck nest new nib nil nine nice no nod nor not now nose next nail note nun neat noon notice none nugget numb nappy near nearly never night noodle nothing number noise north needle nobody nutty nurse naughty normal November noisy narrow native nature nasty newspaper nineteen ninety notice napkin narrative nasal nation nationality nativity naval navigate nectar negative neglect negligent neigh neighbor nursery neighborhood neither nerve nervous neutral neutron newt nasturtium nitrogen noble nocturnal nomad nominate nonsense noose northerly novice novel nought naught noxious novelty nuclear nucleus nurture nutcracker nymph nylon nuzzle	bunny sunny funny runny inn innkeeper manner banner planner spanner tanner scanner nanny banning scanning manning fanning panning tanning canning planning spanning skinning pinning spinning grinning thinning skinned pinned grinned thinned winner thinner spinner skinnier dinner inner beginner beginning breadwinner skinny penned tennis shunned gunned sunned hosanna announce announced announcing announcement connect connection reconnect disconnect innocent innocence julienne connive conniving connoisseur	knit knot knack knap knave knee kneed knead kneel knelt knew know knickers knife knives knob knight knighthood knitwear knock knoll knowing knowingly knowledge knuckle knurl	gnat gnarl gnarled gnash gnat gnaw gnawing gnocchi gnome gnu **pn** **pneumonia** pneumonia pneumatic pneumonic

Grapho-phonic Understanding: List Words

Symbol   **Common Spellings of the Sound**

ng	ng song, ring, bang and hung	ngue tongue
	song long dong gong Hong Kong wrong tong along belong strong prong pronged sarong sarongs throng **ring** bring ding king ping ring sing ting wing sting thing fling swing cling sling string spring morning evening going nothing anything something being during pudding stocking clothing beginning hiding lying shining smiling fishing swimming cleaning camping hanging beating raining switching guessing washing flying living hiding licking liking ferrying marrying dripping hugging wagging wetting chugging hoping hopping removing surfing sailing jogging hiking riding running skipping dancing diving skating whistling skiing gingham complaining coloring eyeing injecting changing exchanging supplying **bang** fang gang hang pang rang sang tang twang clang slang sprang language **hung** dung lung rung sung stung flung swung clung slung strung sprung	tongue tongues

o	o hot	a swan	h honest
	hot hog hop hot on bob cot cob cog dog doll dot fox fob fog got hog jog jot job lot lob lock log lop mop mob nob nod pod pox pop pot rob rod rot sob top onto rock not gone hock cross boss floss loss moss toss lock block off frost knot mock jockey jolly goggles volley soggy holiday hospital across body bossy clock cold crop frog gold fobs moth sold upon belong block bottle bottom cloth comic dollar collar follow knock office often orange robber rocket sorry stock stocking strong borrow collar common copy hopped offer police porridge proper socks bomb coffee model toffee toxic doctor	swan was what wash washing washed wander wandered wandering wand wands wad wattle swallow quarry swans wasp wasps swamp swamps watch watched watching squash squashing squashed wallet wallets wallaby wallabies swap swapped swapping swallowed swallowing squabble squad squads squadron squat swat swatting swatted waft quarrel quarrelling quarrelled waddle waddled waddling wafting	honest honestly honesty honor honors honored honoring honorary

ō	oa boat	o–e bone	ow low	o open	oe toe	ough though
	boat boating goat goats coat coated road roads load loading loaded unload foam foaming moan moaner groan groaned soap soapy soak soaking loaf loaves float floating toast toasting boast boasted coach coaching coached approach reproach croaking coaxing	bone stone woke hope rope chose nose close those note broken unbroken awoke stones hopes hoped ropes chosen closes closed notes noted choke dose doze globe spoke spoken telephone cone throne prone tone zone froze quote quoted backbone wishbone vote voted rode joke joked joker smoke smoker alone wrote stroke rose code mode forebode explode erode evoke invoke provoke ozone hopeless homeless postpone microphone xylophone suppose	low bow snow flow grow show row tow grow crow slow own know yellow window arrow below tomorrow burrow borrow rainbow known blown grown thrown shown owner ownership owned grown follow follows followed following pillow fellow aglow bungalow overflow outgrow scarecrow bestow stowed elbow unknown snowy	so no go also ago both most open over overs only mostly almost hello won't don't opal opening opened opener pony ponies bony nobody outgo post posting posted cargo comb combing combed ghost ghostly grocer hotel soda motor chosen frozen bulldozer motorist notice notices ocean lotion motion notion potion emotion devotion October November piano poem postage potato tomato radio video zero rodeo studio folio polo solo embryo indigo vertigo buffalo placebo diploma aroma coma omen osmosis hypnosis erosive rogue vogue cologne yodel folk yolk honeycomb chromosome	toe doe floe hoe goes roe woe oboe joey hoeing woes woeful tiptoe tiptoeing toed cargoes potatoes tomatoes **ew** **sew** sew sews sewed sewn unsewn	though dough doughy **eau** **beau** bureau trousseau plateau chateau **oo** **brooch** brooch brooches **eo** **yeoman** yeoman

Grapho-phonic Understanding: Word Lists

ô	a **ball**	aw **paw**	or **fork**	au **sauce**	oor **door**
	ball tall call fall hall mall wall stall small smaller smallest taller tallest baseball basketball football rainfall snowfall nightfall squall recall recalling recalled appalling appalled install installing installed enthrall talk chalk walk stalk walked walker walking talked talker talking chalks stalking stalked jaywalker sleepwalker sleepwalking **sure** surely	paw saw jaw law raw caw dawn lawn fawn pawn draw claw drawn drawl prawn crawl flaw gnaw shawl thaw brawl trawler yawn straw hawk sprawl scrawl pawpaw coleslaw withdraw seesaw dawdle awning **our** **four** four pour your court downpour fourteen fourth course source gourd mourn mourning mourned troubadour **oar** **board** oar oars boar roar soar board aboard sideboard cardboard surfboard springboard chalkboard outboard overboard switchboard hoarse hoard	for horn corn fork born torn worn form sort short sport morning storm corner torch north order organ orchid orchard horse force popcorn report reporting reporter reported forget forgotten fortnight formal normal informal abnormal passport export transport support resort escort forty airport afford format fortnightly fortieth northerly cornering sword fortune adorn forlorn divorce reinforce chord assortment distorted orchard torture scorching uniform thunderstorm scornful newborn	sauce saucer launch autumn laundry astronaut August faucet haul maul dinosaur daunt daunting undaunted flaunt taunt gauze clause pause cauldron fraud applaud marauding **ar** **war** war warn warning ward award warm awarded awarding reward rewarded rewarding toward towards warmer warmest wardrobe dwarf dwarfs swarm swarming housewarming forewarn warned thwart lukewarm quarter quarterly	door doormat poor poorly floor flooring moor mooring **ore** **more** sore shore tore bore core score more snore pore store wore swore adore before therefore folklore deplore explore ignore carnivore Singapore **ough** **bought** bought thought brought nought fought sought wrought **augh** **taught** taught caught daughter naughty haughty fraught naught slaughter

oi	oi oil	oy boy
	oil boil coil foil coin join point soil soils oiling oiled oiliness boiling boiled coiling coiled uncoil uncoiled uncoiling recoil recoiled recoiling coins coined doily doilies foil foiled foiling groin groins joined joining joint pointed pointing pointless hoist hoisted hoisting moist noise noisily poise poising poised soiled soiling spoil spoiled spoiling spoils unspoiled toil toiling toiled toils broil choice choices voice voices invoice void avoid avoidance typhoid joist tabloid asteroid alkaloid adjoin adjoining sirloin disjoint appoint appointed appointing appointment anoint anointed anointing viewpoint rejoice disjointed pinpointed moisture moisturize disjointed	boy boys toy toys toying toyed joy joys enjoy enjoyed enjoying enjoyment royal employ destroy disloyalty royalty voyage voyages joyful voyaged voyaging ploy ploys employs employed employing employment employer unemployed unemployment corduroy annoy annoyed annoying alloy alloys destroyed destroying destroyer

Grapho-phonic Understanding: Word Lists

Symbol   Common Spellings of the Sound

ou			
	ou **house**	**ow** **cow**	**ough** **bough**
	out our ours ouch house houses housed housing mouse about trout blouse shout shouting shouted cloud clouds cloudy outing mouth count counted counting counter counts loud loudly aloud south sound proud scout pout spout sprout thousand mountain amount couch pouch grouch crouch foul lout proudly sounds sounded sounding bound hound mound pound round around ground sound wound surround background rebound ounce bounce pounce flounce spouse louse noun pronoun thousands thousandth mountains mountainous fountain fountains clubhouse guardhouse lighthouse storehouse penthouse dugout blackout knockout lookout without throughout roundabout roust about dumbfounded astounded surrounding bouncing announcing doubt doubted doubting grout grouting	cow cows how now vow sow owl owls crown down fowl fowls brown clown clowns crowd crown frown town gown power howl howling howls howled clowning crowds crowded crowding crowns crowned crowning downstairs flower flowers shower tower sunflower drown drowns drowning drowned growl growling growled growls towel towels scowl scowling prowl prowling towelling somehow anyhow eyebrow highbrow allow allows allowance disallow powder powdering powered powders power powers gown nightgown downtown chowder gunpowder dowel trowel empowered powerless endow	bough boughs plough ploughs ploughing ploughed

p		
	p **pup**	**pp** **puppy**
	pup pip pop pad pan pat peg pen pet pig pin pit pod pot put pie paw pay pea par pace pack page paid pail pain pair pale park part pawn peak peal pear peck peek peel peer pest pick pile pill pink pint pipe pity poem poet poke pole pond pool poor pore pork port post pour puff pull pulp pump pupa purr push paint panda panic panel pansy pants pinch pure pew pass past path palm paper party pasta paste patio pause peace peach pearl pecan pedal penal petal piano piece pygmy pitch pizza poach point polar polio pouch pound power punch pulse purse packet paddle pyjamas palace pantry parcel pardon parent parrot pastel pastry patrol pawpaw peanut pebble peddle pelvic people pepper person pickle picnic pigeon piglet pigsty pillow pimple pirate pocket poetry poison police policy polish polite poodle possum postal poster potato potion powder public puddle pumice purely purple pursue puzzle Pacific package paddock padlock pageboy painful pancake panicky papoose papyrus parsley parsnip partner passage passion pastime pasture patella patient pattern payment peacock peasant pelican pendant penguin pensive percent perfect perform perfume pergola perhaps perjury pianist piccolo picture pigment pitiful polenta pollute polygon popcorn popular portion possess postage posture pottery poultry poverty powdery puberty publish pudding pumpkin puritan purpose pursuit putting pyramid pacifist painless paintbox palatial pamphlet pancreas panicked panpipes paradise paraffin parallel paralyze parasite parental particle passport password pastoral pastries pathetic patience pavement payphone peaceful peculiar pedigree pentagon perceive personal perspire persuade pictures pipeline pointing politely ponytail pondweed populate porpoise porridge portable porthole portrait position positive possible possibly postcard postmark postpone poultice powerful publican publicly punctual punctuation puncture purchase	puppy puppies apple apples happy happier happiest happiness unhappy puppet puppets pepper popped popping slipped slipper slippers slipping skipped skipping clippings clipped strapped strapping unstrapping unstrapped tripping tripped hopped hopping dripped dripping zapped zapping chopped chopping zipper zipped supply supplying supplied supplies unhappily puppetry wrapping wrapped approach approached appear appearance disappear disappearance approve approval apprehend apprehended apprehension apparel apparatus apparent appendix appetite appetizer applaud applause applied appointment application appliance appreciate apply appreciation approximate approximately apprehensive

Grapho-phonic Understanding: Word Lists

Symbol   Common Spellings of the Sound

r		
r **run**	**rr** **carry**	**wr** **wrong**
run ran rag ram rat red rib rid rig rim rip rob rod rot rub rug raw ray row race rack raft rent rice rich ride rind ring ripe rise risk road roar robe rode role roll roof room root rope rose ruck ruin rink riot rule rung rust rage raid rail rain raindrop raincoat rainfall rainproof river roast rocks rake ramp rang rank rate rave raze read real rear reed reef reel ranch rein rely runny rusty right rinse ripen risky rocky rodeo rough round rover royal rugby races radar radio rainy raise rally range ribbon rubbish riddle ripple robbed robber rocket rodent roping rotten royalty rubber rapid rayon ratio razor reach react ready rifle rabbit racket raccoon raffle ramble ranger rapids reflect reform refuel refund regards remain remake remote remove rental repeat replay rescue resign resume retell retire return review reward remember racquet railway rainbow rapidly ravioli readily realize receipt receive recount recover recruit recycle referee reflect refresh refusal regular rejoice release removal require reserve resolve respect respond restore reunion revolve rewound rivalry robbery rookery roughly reaction reassign regiment register regulate rehearse reindeer relations relative reminder renovate renovations restrain	carry carries carried carrying carriage hurry hurried hurries hurrying ferry ferried ferries ferrying merry merrily carrot carrots barrel barrels furry marry married marries marrying lorry lorries worry worried worries worrying tomorrow arrow error errors barrow wheelbarrow narrow narrowed narrowing narrowly borrow borrowed borrowing burrow burrowed burrowing correct corrected correcting correction porridge terror terrible terrific terrify horror horrific horrible cherry cherries berry berries quarry quarried quarries quarrel quarreling quarrelsome	wrong wrangle wrap wreck wreckage wrong wrongly wrecking wren wrist write written writer writing unwritten wrote wrench wrestle wrapped wrapping wrapper wreath wriggle wring wrung wringer wrinkle wrinkly wrath wraith wrack playwright writhe wrought **rh** **rhyme** rhyme rhythm rhythmic rhubarb rhombus rhinoceros rheumatic rhesus rhetoric rhapsody

s				
s **sick**	**ss** **miss**	**c** **cent, circus and cycle**	**sc** **science**
sick so see sea sum sun set sell seen seem said says self saw sale sang sent seal seven sir sister soft sold safe sail some son song soap soil sort sound south silk size soak summer school somebody sometime something someone salt Saturday season second September sew sight silly silver since soldier sore sorry sudden Sunday sunny supper surprise safety sailor saucer search secret sentence settle seventeen seventy sigh sign signal silent simple sixteen sixty socks soup subject suppose suit sandwich suddenly surprised sarong satire savage savory seldom sequel series simply sizzle solemn somber sonnet sorrow sought subdue submit suburb sugary summit sunken superb symbol siphon system salvage sarcasm sausage seaweed seasick secrecy section segment selfish senator sensory several similar	miss hiss kiss bliss cross boss toss floss gross loss moss lass mass dress less mess fuss bass across class glass grass pass brass press lesson guess princess address sickness illness message unless useless dresses chess bless stress grasses harass hourglass compass trespass happiness heaviness readiness painless fairness careless airless stainless weightless spotless underpass overpass thankless harassing seamless needless fearless confess caress headdress undress distress success possess repossess priceless readdressed essence successor relentless thickness confession recession excessive kindness lifeless wireless admission	cent cement rice mice dice fence prince lace princess celery place palace dance ambulance dunce space mace price centipede century cell cellar parcel cereal cancel cancer police trace notice replace since office officer peace piece twice sentence voice balance certain certainly chance chances grocer grocery groceries decide except exception receive deceive **circus** city cigar pencil cinders icicle circle cicada cider cinema council cinnamon citric cipher cistern citizen civic civil civilian civilized civilization citrus incinerator circa circled circular circuit circulate circulation circumference **cycle** bicycle tricycle fancy icy cymbal cyclist juicy cyclone cylinder cyst cynic encyclopedia	science scissors scent scents scented abscess ascent descent scene scenery scientific disciple muscle muscles fascinate resuscitate discipline sceptre miscellaneous convalescent adolescent reminiscent **ps** **psychology** psychology pseudonym psalm psychiatry psychic psychological **st** **listen** listen whistle castle wrestle rustle glisten thistle mistletoe

Grapho-phonic Understanding: Word Lists

Symbol   Common Spellings of the Sound

sh	**sh** **ship**	**ci** **special**	**ti** **station**	**ch** **machine**
	ship shot shop she shift shelf shut shack shock sheet sheep fish dish wish cash dash mash rash rush brush show shown shake shape shirt shone shine shade shark shoe shoot sharp shell shout shave shame shrub shingle shiver shore shadow shallow shining shiny shorten shower shawl shoelace shopping shipment posh mush leash wash bush shredded sheik mushroom shoulder shrapnel shameful	special social magician official sufficient efficient electrician politician physician technician optician musician suspicion gracious spacious vicious delicious suspicious **ce** **ocean** ocean oceanic oceanarium oceanography	station relation option attention position information examination preparation consideration description condition partition ambition addition tradition edition audition ignition nutrition tuition evaluation ambitious nutritious fictitious **si** **tension** tension pension excursion concussion discussion admission remission omission permission transmission emission	machine machinery brochure moustache champagne chauffeur chateau chalet chef **sci** **conscience** conscience conscientious **s** **sure** sure surely surety issue tissue

t	**t** **tap**	**tt** **button**	**ed** **tapped**
	tap ten tin ton tag tip tea tee tent tank tall tack tail tale take tape to too two table tie tick time today team torch tile tool tomorrow tonight ticket tiny tied tired tear tow toe television terrible together touch taste teach taught telephone timber tennis tease tight tomato toast towards towel tough tire tooth teeth tongue topic typical temperature temperament temptation	kitten letter little button better getting pretty prettier prettiest bottle bottom cattle battle matter written kettle forgotten settle rattle settlement embattlement **th** **Thomas** Thomas Thai Thailand thyme	bumped rushed brushed flashed crunched camped jumped stamped stumped barked thanked kicked walked talked hooked cooked looked stalked washed locked reached watched washed danced braked piped voiced joked smoked faced raced placed spaced hiked fenced nursed iced sliced strapped tapped snapped slipped cropped tripped hiked laughed unmarked remarked unlaced unlocked

th	**th** **thin**
	thin thick thug third thank thong thorn thing think thrill thirsty thought thousand theft threw through thumb Thursday thief thump throne thicken thinner thunder thigh thrown throat thread thrift throb throw death breath tooth teeth north south mouth youth month truth bath path thermal thundery thankful thorough thorny thorax theory sleuth mouthful thirteen thirty fourth fifth sixth seventh eighth ninth tenth twentieth thirtieth fortieth fiftieth sixtieth seventieth eightieth ninetieth hundredth thyroid thesis these myth goldsmith blacksmith

TH	**th** **then**	**the** **breathe**
	then the than them they that this there their they're those these themselves therefore though	breathe bathe lathe feather weather leather

U	**u** **mug**	**o** **come**	**ou** **double**	**oo** **flood**
	mug mud gun sun sum fuzz buzz bump dull luck hunt dust lunch brush funny bunny puppy summer bunch hunch butter sudden number hurry hundred hungry bubble buckle button public crumb dumb lucky study husband jungle tunnel	come some done son won wonder coming honey money front Monday London monkey shovel dozen sponge none color love glove dove shove above other another brother mother smother compass nothing tongue cover discover grandson does doesn't	double couple young cousin trouble tough rough enough youngest younger country countries touch touched touching untouchable	flood blood flooding flooded bloody

Grapho-phonic Understanding: Word Lists

Symbol   **Common Spellings of the Sound**

u	oo **book**	u **full**	ou **could**
	book look took cook hook nook rook brook crook shook soot wood good hood stood wool rookery woollen lambswool woolly plywood firewood driftwood barefoot cookbook unhook outlook manhood womanhood knighthood	full pull bull **put** fully pulley bully wishful dreadful watchful helpful glassful mouthful grateful hopeful faithful graceful	would should couldn't wouldn't shouldn't o **wolf** wolf

ü	oo **moon**	ew **screw**	ui **fruit**	ou **croup**
	moon soon room noon root hoot boot shoot cool pool tool fool roof spoon brood broom balloon groom bedroom bridegroom zoom taboo bamboo shampoo igloo kangaroo tattoo proof fireproof foolproof whirlpool toadstool school choose snooze classroom balloonist cartoonist **ough** **through** through throughout	screw threw drew blew flew chew crew jewel grew brew slew withdrew mildew corkscrew unscrew thumbscrew jewelery **u** **rule** rule June dune prune flume flute brute pollute salute longitude latitude solitude magnitude molecule truth gnu Zulu jury juror humor rumor tumor mural plural rural	fruit juice fruity fruited breadfruit juicy juiced juicing suit lawsuit pursuit recruit recruited bruise cruise cruiser cruising **oe** **shoe** shoe shoes canoe canoes horseshoe horseshoes **ue** **blue** blue true flue glue clue untrue gruesome chop suey	croup tour touring toured caribou ghoul coup tourist troupe coupe route mousse **o** **who** who do to ado redo outdo into movie movement tomb womb whom

v	v **van**			f **of**
	van vat vet vent vast veal vest vine vale vain vein **vane** vow vowel vary vase vile vial vice view visa void vault volt vote vamp via valid vague value valve venom virus visit vivid visor voltage voice vomit venue verge verse video vinyl viola vitamin volcano vacant vacate vacuum valley vapor velvet violet violin vision visual volleyball volume voyage vampire vanilla vantage vapors varnish vehicle venture veteran victory village vinegar violent **vacancy vaguely violate volcanic vicious verify** vineyard verandah venomous vegetable vendor verbal viable vibes valuable vacation voucher vulture			of ph **Stephen** Stephen

w	w **will**	u **quick**
	will win wag wax way wed well wind wood web wife wig wow went wing wink wake ward wave weep woke wire wise weak week worn walk want warn wasp wand wash watch window winter water word war wore would warm wart wear ware whether weather Wednesday wild wolf wonder was worm waxy wages waste waist weekly weakly weigh weight welcome western weakness westward wetlands wicked witch woman women widow widower worldly woollen womanly weekday weekend worry worth wives wedding womb waltz wiggle wound wanderer wardrobe weary weave wedge warranty weird widen waterbed wealthy worse worst worth wisdom warfare warrant waffle wallet weapon warrior wastage walnut walrus wizard wander warmth wilderness wattle wobble wombat wolves worsen withdraw withdrawal **wh** **wheat** wheat wheel whale whip why while white which when what where whereas whether whirl whiff whistle wharf whirligig whirlwind wharves wheeze wheezy whisk whisker whisper whim whimper whelk overwhelm whelp whippet whet whittle whiz whey	quick quack queen quad quit quiz quilt quintuplet equip quail quake earthquake queer quest quiet quite quote **quota** quirk quaint quarry quiver qualm quality qualify quarrel quarter quill quicken quickly quantity quarters question quotient quotation quagmire quadrant squid squelch squeal squeeze square squaw squint **o** **choir** choir

Grapho-phonic Understanding: Word Lists

Symbol	Common Spellings of the Sound

x	x **box** box fox pox ox fix six mix pix ax wax tax flax taxi chickenpox smallpox strongbox jukebox pillbox hatbox chatterbox paradox orthodox relax beeswax climax pickax fixture mixture prefix suffix crucifix annex duplex complex index reflex perplex	cks **socks** socks locks docks rocks backs kicks licks ducks trucks clocks ticks sticks knocks shocks stocks blocks packs smacks tracks tacks snacks cracks quacks slacks picks tricks chicks flicks bricks plucks checks necks decks pecks specks wrecks shipwrecks paperbacks quarterbacks racetracks haversacks haystacks matchsticks throwbacks knicknacks woolpacks

y	y **yes** yes yell yap yam yet you your yours you're yellow youth yard yelp yarn yawn yoga year yoke yolk yesterday young yummy yo-yo yourself yield yacht years yeast yearly yonder youthful yearn yellowy yogurt younger youngest youngish yearbook yearling	i **opinion** opinion opinionated j **hallelujah** hallelujah

yü	you **you** you you've youth youthful yu **yule** Yuletide eue **queue** queue eau **beauty** beauty beautiful	ew **few** few stew knew new renew skewer pew hewn dew iew **view** view viewed viewing review ieu **adieu** adieu lieu	u **use** use fuse bugle mule cube tube tune mute cute fume ue **cue** cue due subdue avenue revenue duel fuel eu **feud** feud Zeus

z	z **zero** zip zoo whiz zoom quiz zero zebra zipper zoological zoology zigzag zap zeal zenith zinc zest zone zonal zucchini zz **buzz** buzz fizz fuzz dizzy frizzy fizzle drizzle frizzle sizzle	s **has** has as is his busy prison present imprison peasant chisel resident president prism journalism criticism hypnotism flimsy whimsy ss **scissors** scissors x **xylophone** xylophone

zh	s **measure** measure pleasure treasure leisure measuring leisurely treasured ge **garage** garage	si **division** division television decision collision erosion confusion conclusion transfusion elusion illusion explosion exclusion revision z **azure** azure

Linking Consonant Word Lists

Initial Links

tr **trap**	trap trip trod trot trim tramp tree try tray track trade trail train trust trick tribe troll trout tread trophy truck true transport traffic tricycle triple triceratops triceps tribunal tribal tricolor trilingual
pr **pram**	pram prod prick print press prize price prickle proof prince princess pray prey prayer pretty prune praise problem prance prefer practice president produce protein protective protocol provide provoke
cr **crab**	crab cram crept cry crust crack cramp crust cross crash creep creeper crane crowd crumb craft crazy crown crew cream cricket cradle crime credit criminal criticism crater crocodile creature creative crevasse
dr **drum**	drum dress drill dry drip draft drag drop drink draw drain dream drug drown dragon drove drone dray dribble drizzle drawer drumstick dreary drowsy drought drama drudgery
fr **from**	from fresh frog frost frank fry front frown fruit free freedom frame friend freeze freckle frozen fracture fright frighten fractions fraud France French freight frequent frequently
br **bread**	brim brat brick brush brown brook bread brake breeze branch break brain breed breast brave bright brass brood brother broken breathe bridge bridle bridal brief British broad
gr **grin**	grin grab green greet great grown groan grape grain grand grow grumpy graph grass grandmother grandfather grasshopper grave grind ground graze grease grief grateful grieve grouch grocery Greece
sk **skip**	skip skid sky skate skin skim skill skunk skeleton ski skies skirt skipper skunk skull sketch skateboard skein skewer skirmish skyscraper skylight
st **step**	step stop stem stick star stack stab stag stand stamp stiff still sting stitch stir story stock start state stale stain stay stun steam storm stone steer store stalk stage stable stew stocking stadium staff stretcher starfish steel steal stair stare steady stump stomach stern storey stony sterilize stereotype status
fl **flag**	flag flat flap flip fly float fling flesh flea flake flame flick flash flock flask flavor flower flour flow flute flutter fluid floor flight flyover fluid flume fluorescent fluoride
sp **spot**	spot spin spun spell spit spend speck spine spice space spill speech spoil spout sport spoon spade spite spider sponge spear spirit special spike speculate species sponsorship spouse spoken spokesperson
tw **twig**	twig twin twist twice twirl twister twitch twinkle twiddle twenty twelve twelfth twentieth twilight twinge twinkling twitter twisted
sw **swim**	swim sweep swell swift sweep swept swing swipe swirl swoop swear sweat switch swan swallow swamp swab swarm swivel swat swimming swollen sway sweepstakes sweltering Swiss swindle swivel
cl **clap**	clay clip clam cliff club clog clock clown clamp cloud clever close clear clean clinic class clutter clap climate clothes cluster clinical climb climax cloister clover clue client
bl **blob**	blob blank blink blend bless black bleed block blow bloom blush bluff bliss blue blood blind blast bloat blanket blame blaze blizzard blur blossom blistering blubber blouse blunder blockade
gl **glad**	glad glee glum glut gloss glen glow glass glance gleam glory glamour glacier gland glassy glide glider globe gloom glorious glorify gloomy glowing glucose glamorous glacier glacial global gladiator
pl **plug**	plug plum plan plant play please plate plane planes plain planet place ply pledge plight plaster plastic plumber platform platoon pleasure pleasant pliers pledge pliable
sl **slip**	slip slop slap slump slab slug slant sling slept sleep sled sleepy slice slide slope slow slush slumber sly slender slippery slippers sloppy slime slimy slave sleepily slouch slither slogan slumber slur
sc **scab**	scab scar scarf scoot scoop scooter scare scarecrow scatter scalp scales scone scold score scorpion scandal scalpel sculpt sculpture
sn **snow**	snap snug sniff snail snoop snake snow sneeze sneak snorkel snuggle snowball snowflake snowfall snow snowshoes snout snore snooze
sm **small**	small smell smart smile smoke smack smash smooth smelt smoky smother smudge smuggle smear smatter smarten smiley smoking smokeless smolder smorgasbord
str **string**	strip string strain strap straw stream street streak stripe stretch strike stride structure strong strut strewn stress straight strength struggle strategy stratosphere
spr **sprint**	sprig sprint sprain sprite sprang spread spray sprawl spree spruce sprung sprinkler sprinkle sprout springbok springboard sprightly sprocket spruce
thr **three**	three thrill throne thrown throat throb thrust throw thrive thrift thread threat thrash throaty throng threw threat threaten through throughout thrush throttle thrombosis
scr **scrap**	scrap scrub scream scrape scribble script screech screen scratch scratchy screw scribe scripture scrimp scruples scroll scrabble
spl **splash**	splint split splat splinter splash splashing spleen splice splendid splutter splintery splendor splay

Linking Consonant Word Lists

Final Links

st **best**	best west list mist must dust gust rust bust test nest chest wrest guest frost host most coast post roast toast boast burst first mast prettiest loneliest naughtiest calmest noisiest sportiest
nt **bent**	bent sent went spent gent lent dent ant plant grant pant lint mint hint tint faint feint point anoint joint amount want front pint independent superintendent improvement assistant resistant resident accountant brilliant constant entrant immigrant incompetent inconsistent indent non-existent payment pleasant servant transplant
mp **jump**	jump bump lump hump camp stamp lamp damp limp sump trump tramp romp stump cramp stomp revamp
ft **lift**	lift left loft sift gift soft drift cleft rift adrift aloft
ld **hold**	held hold told cold fold bold gold sold field yield shield meld weld mold
sk **desk**	desk risk tusk brisk ask task mask cask bask flask frisk disk whisk
sp **wisp**	rasp clasp grasp lisp wisp wasp
nd **land**	and land sand band hand wind end bend lend mend send find hind kind rind wind grind fond bond found ground hound mound pound round around sound wand wound
lt **belt**	belt felt melt colt malt salt halt cult adult pelt welt fault built guilt
ct **act**	act fact duct enact affect effect precinct

Compound Lists

Newspapers are a great source of compound words. Many students can have a lot of success spelling these words because they can see the two smaller words within them.

afternoon	aircraft	airtight	anybody	anyone	anything	anytime	anyway
anywhere	backdrop	background	backward	baseball	basketball	bathroom	bedroom
bedspread	below	beside	birthdate	birthday	birthplace	blackboard	blackout
blindfold	bookcase	bookmark	boyfriend	breakfast	butterfly	campsite	childhood
copyright	crossword	database	daytime	deadline	desktop	doorbell	download
downpour	downstairs	dragonfly	evergreen	everybody	everyone	everything	everytime
everywhere	eyebrow	farmhouse	farmyard	feedback	fingernail	fireproof	flashback
flashbulb	floorboard	football	footprint	forgave	forgive	forward	friendship
girlfriend	goodbye	grandchild	grandparent	graveyard	greenhouse	greyhound	guesswork
guidebook	guideline	haircut	hairstyle	hallway	handcraft	handstand	handwriting
handwritten	hardware	heartache	heartbeat	herself	highlight	highway	himself
homework	indoor	inside	into	keyboard	keyword	knockout	landslide
legroom	lifeboat	lifesaver	lifestyle	lighthouse	lipstick	livestock	lunchtime
matchbox	maybe	meanwhile	moonbeam	moonlight	motorbike	nestegg	network
newsletter	newspaper	nickname	nightmare	nightwear	nobody	notebook	nothing
offshore	online	onto	otherwise	outdated	outdoor	outside	overnight
overseas	paperback	password	photocopy	piggyback	playground	postcard	racetrack
rainbow	roadwork	saltwater	seafood	seashell	shareholder	shoelace	showroom
skydive	softball	software	somebody	somehow	someone	sometimes	somewhere
songwriter	soundproof	spaceship	spotlight	spreadsheet	starfish	stockbroker	storyboard
Sunday	sunflower	sunray	sunshine	superhuman	teapot	teardrop	timetable
today	tonight	toolbox	toothbrush	toothpaste	tracksuit	trademark	treetop
typeface	typeset	undergo	underground	understand	update	upon	upstairs
videotape	waistcoat	waterfall	website	weekend	wetsuit	wheelbarrow	whenever
whiteboard	whoever	windscreen	windsurf	without	workshop	worldwide	worthwhile

Greek and Latin Word Origin Lists

This may encourage the students to seek more information about the origin of words.

Greek	"aero" meaning "air"	"autos" meaning "self"	"photo" meaning "light"	"tele" meaning "far"
	aerosol	autograph	photograph	televise
	aerodrome	automatic	photographer	television
	aerobic	automobile	photographic	telethon
	aerobics	automate	photography	telecast
	aerospace	autobiography	photocopy	telecommunication
	aerofoil	autopsy	photocopier	telephone
	aerodynamic	autonomy	photocopies	telegraph
	aeronautical	autonomous	photon	telescope
	aerogramme	**"scope" meaning "look"**	photomural	telepathy
	"hydro" meaning "water"	microscope	photosphere	teleconference
	hydroelectric	telescope	photosynthesis	telebanking
	hydroelectricity	periscope	photosynthesize	
	hydrofoil	stethoscope	**"phono" meaning "voice"**	
	hydrogen	**"geo" meaning "earth"**	microphone	
	hydrometer	geography	saxophone	
	hydroplane	geocentric	xylophone	
		geographical	megaphone	
		geology	phonogram	
			telephone	

Latin	"aqua" meaning "water"	"video" meaning "see"	"multi" meaning "much, many"	"uni" meaning "one"
	aquatic	video	multiply	unit
	aqueous	videotape	multiple	unicycle
	aquarium	videoconference	multiplication	unicorn
	aquamarine	video recorder	multicultural	universe
	aqualung	videotext	multilingual	uniform
	aqueduct	**"radio" meaning "ray, beam"**	multinational	union
	aquifer	radio	multicolored	unify
	Aquarius	radioactive	multilayered	unison
	aquarobics	radiology	multilevel	unique
	"annus" meaning "year"	radiotherapy	multimedia	unite
	annual	radiographer	multiform	**"bi" meaning "two"**
	annually	radiocarbon	multitude	bicycle
	annuity	radiogenic	multimillion	bicentenary
	"audio" meaning "hear"	radiograph	multimillionaire	bicentennial
	audiologist			biceps
	auditory			bicolor
	audition			bicuspid
	audit			**"tri" meaning "three"**
	audiophone			tricycle
				triangle
				tricolor
				trilogy
				tricuspid
				trident

Class Activities for Use with Phonic Family Word Lists

Class Activities

On the following pages are suggestions of how to use the phonic family word lists in different class activities. All these activities can be adapted to the level of your students by using either the blue, green or red list of words and phonic sounds. Refer to the lists on pages 21 – 38.

Storytelling 45
Alliteration 45
What's Missing – Digraphs 46
Look, Say, Cover, Write, Check – List Words 46
Look, Say, Cover, Write, Check – Dictation 46
Word Search 47
Crossword Puzzles 47
What am I? – Letter Clues 47
What Sound Comes Next? 47
Expand a Sentence 48
What am I? – Meaning of Words in Clues 48
Jumbled Words 48
Homonyms 48
Antonyms 48
Synonyms 49
Word for the Day 49
Brainstorming Sound Families 49
Paragraph Puzzle 49
Look, Say, Cover, Write, Check – Word Building 50
What's Missing – Digraphs/Blends/Consonants 51
Phonic Bingo 51
Across the Curriculum – English/Science/Maths 52
Common Elements – Prefixes/Suffixes/Root Words 52
What's Missing? – Contractions 52
Spoonerisms 52
Across the Curriculum – Reading Text/Decoding Sound Families 53
Word Jumbles 54
Add a Word 54
Interest Words 54
Word Sorts 55
Forgetful Syllables 55
Sporting Puzzles 56
Across the Curriculum – Writing/Spelling/History 56
Research Table 56
Across the Curriculum – Extracting Information/History 56

Class Activities

Storytelling

- When making the students aware of a particular sound, introduce that sound by using words from the lists for storytelling (e.g., "ar" – car list of words). Make the story as imaginative and interesting as possible.

- For the story choose words from the lists at your particular class' or individual students' level. This approach allows for a systematic development through the spelling phases.

- After listening to the story, encourage the students to brainstorm all the words they have heard from the story containing that particular sound. Print or write the words on a chart for referral in later activities. Highlight the spelling of the particular sound being treated in a different color, so the students will see the sound–symbol association. Read these charted words with the students and play appropriate games with them. (These games will depend on the age level of the students.)

- Students may then use these words in their own storytelling or writing activities and decoding exercises to consolidate the sound. The spelling pattern for this sound will become more familiar if the students are bombarded with it in print form.

- Depending on the phases of development of the student, compare other known spellings of this particular sound (e.g., "ar" car, "a" bath, "ear" heart, "au" laugh, "er" sergeant) and form class lists for each family of words. Students could spontaneously add to these lists from material they read during their daily work.

Alliteration

A fun activity is to use the lists of words provided for initial sounds and challenge the students to make up lines of alliteration to read back to the other students. Model this with younger students and chart group or class efforts before they attempt their own piece of alliteration. For example:

My Mom Makes Me Muffins

Dad Digs Dams Deep

Football Fever For Family

Peter Peered Past Plump Panda Painted Poster

An Athletic Ant Admired An African Antelope Across Arid Africa

Cold Country Castles Caused Carol's Cough

Class Activities

What's Missing? – Digraphs

On the chalkboard, write a word with a missing sound and leave the word on the board until someone guesses the missing sound and spells the word correctly. For example:

str __ __ t (ee)   str __ __ __ __t (aigh)   str __ __ mer (ea)

str __ __n (ai)   str __ p __ (i–e)   n __ __ __ __ b __ __ (eigh/or)

Look, Say, Cover, Write, Check – List Words

Students look and say, then cover, write and check a list of words.

Look Cover Check

Did you get it right? If you did, give yourself a check. If you didn't, try again.

cable	yesterday
data	away
input	belt
output	felt
disc	seal
save	real
spray	fear
bay	year
today	hear

BIG Effort: You can make new words by adding 's'.

cables   discs   saves   sprays   bays   belts   seals   fears   years   hears
Can you read these words? You may like to learn to spell them also.

Look, Say, Cover, Write, Check – Dictation

Make up dictation for the students based on a list of words being treated. Students read and cover, then copy the sentence and check their spelling.

Dictation

1. Save your money today for when we go away.
2. Plug in the cable and input the data into the computer.
3. My job yesterday was to spray the weeds.
4. I felt happy to see the seal swim in the bay.
5. It took me one year to pass my black belt in judo.

BIG effort: Make up your own sentences.

Class Activities

Word Search

- When making up a word search, include a secret message for the students. This motivates them to find all the words to get to the secret message.

- Once the student has found the nominated words, CAKE, PLACE, SPACE, GRAPE, SAFE, TALE, ACE, the remaining letters left to right, top to bottom, form the secret message. In this case, "I think you have done very well!".

I	P	T	H	I	N	K
C	Y	L	O	U	A	H
A	S	A	A	V	C	T
K	P	E	D	C	E	A
E	A	S	O	N	E	L
E	C	V	A	E	R	E
Y	E	W	E	F	L	L
G	R	A	P	E	E	!

Secret Message: ___   ___ ___ ___ ___ ___

___ ___ ___

___ ___ ___ ___

___ ___ ___ ___

___ ___ ___ ___

___ ___ ___ ___

Crossword Puzzles

- Before a class or group is given a crossword puzzle, use the clues for an oral quiz. Each group of six students, for example, works as a team and is given one point for guessing the correct word and one point for correct spelling. This motivates the students and helps focus weaker spellers' thoughts when they need to read the crossword clues independently later in the lesson.

What am I? – Letter Clues

Example: thought

- I have 7 letters.
- I have 2 vowels and 5 consonants.
- I have 2 letter "h" and 2 letter "t" but I only have one "th" sound.

  Students could make up their own set of three clues to share with their group. Always model this activity initially, so the outcomes of the exercise are very clear.

What Sound Comes Next?

This game is similar to "Hangman".

Write on the chalkboard the format: H ___ ___ ___ ___ ___ ___ ___ ___

Could be _____   Couldn't be _____

- Object of game: Choose the word you want practiced; students need to guess single letters to build up the word.

- Challenge: Students need to come up with the possible correct letter combinations from left to right before you finish drawing a rocket blasting off, for example. This game is more effective than "Hangman" as the students have to apply their knowledge.

- Take, for example, the word "happiness". If a student guesses "h, e", ask for an example, such as "h, e" as in helper. "Yes, it could be that, but it isn't" and you would place "he" on the "Could be" line. If the student had guessed "h, z", you would ask for the word he/she was thinking about and the student would realize it wasn't a possible letter combination, so you would write it down on the "Couldn't be" line. The game continues until the word is made or the drawing is completed.

Class Activities

Expand a Sentence

- Give the class a list of words or brainstorm the list using the sound/sounds you are treating. For example: "oa" boat, "ow" low, "o–e" bone, "o" open, "oe" toe.

  Joe toe broke lonely alone yellow radio video open over pillow stove roast toast soap road rope joker nose telephone pony both goes potatoes hotel nobody

- Write a simple sentence on the chalkboard: Joe broke his toe.

- The students expand the sentence, building it up one or two words at a time, printing it each time.

  Lonely Joe broke his toe.   Lonely Joe broke his yellow toe.
  Lonely homeless Joe broke his yellow toe.   Lonely homeless Joe broke his yellow toe on a radio.

What am I? – Meaning of Words in Clues

I am made of metal.   ___ ___ ___ ___ ___

I take what is not mine.   ___ ___ ___ ___ ___

I am used when fishing.   ___ ___ ___ ___

I am true.   ___ ___ ___ ___

I am a red vegetable.   ___ ___ ___ ___

I am used in musical timing.   ___ ___ ___ ___

In this example long vowel "e" words which are also homonyms have been used (steel, steal, reel, real, beet, beat).

Jumbled Words

Use the list words to make jumbled words in context.

In my lunch box I had **amh** sandwiches and an **ppela**. (ham, apple)

The **ndiw** was **wlingho** across the **orharb**. (wind, howling, harbor)

Bmhooyecn ttseas so good. (Honeycomb, tastes)

Homonyms

- Homonym Puzzles: Fill in the correct words.

  Across: 1. Dogs wag this
           3. Ships set ___.
  Down: 1. A story
        2. The house is for ___.

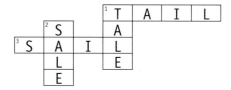

Antonyms

- Antonym Fun:

  Change the context of the sentence: Creeping through the jungle I met an angry lion
                                  Running through the desert I met a happy lion.

  Change the wording so context stays the same: Formal dress code applicable.
                                    Informal dress code inapplicable.

Class Activities

Synonyms

- Synonym Kick-off:

How many synonyms can you put through the goal? The student writes down a word of similar meaning to a given word and scores a goal. Use words from the lists that are appropriate to your outcomes; e.g., when making students aware of the "g" gentle/"g" giant sound, have the students find synonyms.

For example: motor–engine, man–gent, platform–stage.
Use the lists provided on pages 21 – 38 to find words.

Word for the Day

Write a word on the chalkboard early in the day; e.g., technological.

Give a challenge to the class, "By the end of the day see how many different words you can make from the letters used in this word."

Leave 5 – 10 minutes at the end of the day for responses and comparisons.

Brainstorming Sound Families

To brainstorm long vowel "a" words, have the students suggest what the possible spellings could be and make up a chart. Use large sheets of paper and the chalkboard or a whiteboard. Leave lots of room for the students to write their efforts.

"a–e"   "a"   "ay"   "ai"   "ei"   "eigh"

cake   baby   tray   train   rein   neighbor

The class could start to fill in the family of words in the initial lesson and spontaneously add to the lists all day. Reading texts and other materials would act as initiators.

Paragraph Puzzle

Students write a paragraph using a set number of list words. They leave spaces in place of words. Students swap with a friend and try to guess the missing words.

Paragraph Puzzle

Write a paragraph using five of your list words. Leave out the five words you have chosen. Give your paragraph to a friend and see if he or she can guess the missing words.

For example; The <u>children</u> ate their <u>lunches</u> under the shady <u>branches</u> of the tree.

	Guessed Words
_____	_____
_____	_____
_____	_____
_____	_____
_____	_____
_____	

Class Activities

Look, Say, Cover, Write, Check – Spelling/Word Building

Can you sound these list words? Which list words can you spell? Check the ones you can write correctly. If you can spell the list words you may try some or all of the word building list.

List Words	Check	Word Building	Check	Revision	Check
face		faces faced facing			
race		races raced racing			
place		places placed placing			
age		ages aged aging			
cage		cages caged caging			
sale		sales			
tale		tales			
made					
cave		caves			
fork		forks			
cork		corks corked corking uncork			
fort		forts			
horn		horns			
worn		wore			
horse		horses			
birthday		birthdays			
kept		unkept (un means not)			
Mr./Mrs.					

Points to learn:

- Plural (more than one) – add an "s": faces, races, places, ages, cages, sales, tales, caves, corks, forts, horses, horns, birthdays

- Word building homophones – words that sound the same but have a different spelling and a different meaning. For example: made/maid; sale/sail; tale/tail; wore/war; hear/here; horse/hoarse
  Talk about these words and their meanings and write them in a sentence.

- Word building – to make "race" into "racing" we need to drop the "e" and add "ing"

  Spelling rule – when "ing" comes to stay "e" goes away. For example: face/facing; place/placing; age/aging; cage/caging

50   The Complete Phonic Handbook

Class Activities

What's Missing? – Digraphs/Blends/Consonants

Write a word on the chalkboard with sounds missing and leave it until someone guesses the missing sound and spells the whole word.

For example:

____ ____ ____ ow (thr)   ____ ____ ____ ash (spl)

or ____ ____ ar ____ (ch, d)   ____ ____ ____ eam (scr)

____ ____ ____ one (thr)   ____ ____ a ____ ____ ____ oar ____ (ch, lk, b, d)

Phonic Bingo

For one game, you will need to:

- Make up 25 different cards for the class, as below, each with columns B I N G O and five rows of boxes for sounds. Rearrange the sounds in each column by selecting five out of the possible seven sounds of B, then I, then N, G and O until the card is full. You will need two master sheets made up for the game, with the columns B I N G O and seven rows of boxes with all the sounds you want to use on this set of game cards. Keep one sheet whole and cut the other up into individual boxes to be shuffled and selected at random, by you, when the game is played.

- Each student will need a card to play the game and 25 counters or blocks to cover the sounds as you call them out.

- When calling for the game say, clearly: I, "o" for orange, B, "ar" for car, O, "e" for me.

- The first student to cover a designated row, a designated column, or the whole sheet wins points, a sticker or another type of class reward.

- With younger students it is better to highlight the sounds in each row (BINGO) in different colors to help with eye tracking.

- Older and more capable students could make their own set of BINGO cards with your instructions.

- Variations to Phonic Bingo could be to use antonyms, synonyms, homonyms, root words or consonant links.

B	I	N	G	O
"ch" chick	"oo" moon	"i-e" kite	"r" rabbit	"ee" tree
"sh" ship	"oo" book	"i" blind	"wr" wrong	"e" me
"ar" car	"o" pony	"igh" high	"er" mother	"ea" leaf
"tch" watch	"o" orange	"a-e" cake	"ir" bird	"y" happy
"a" bath	"aw" paw	"a" baby	"er" fern	"i" ski
"ck" duck	"or" fork	"a" apple	"ur" church	"ey" key
"k" kitten	"oor" floor	"ai" rain	"ear" pearl	"i-e" machine

Class Activities

Across the Curriculum – English/Science/Math

Silky Worms – Prepare a report on silkworms. (Whole-class effort.)
Make it into a big book. An extra activity to use with the big book could be to decode
"er", "ö", "ë" sounds, as below, from the text.

er	"or"–worm	"ear"–learn "er"–water, bigger, smaller	
ö	"oo"–cocoon	"o"–who "ew"–view	
ë	"ee"–tree, need, needed, see, reel	"ea"–leaf, each, clean, leaves, cleaned	

- Put a triangle around every "er" sound
- Put square around every "ö" sound
- Put a rectangle around every "ë" sound

Common Elements – Prefixes/Suffixes/Root Words

Look for common elements in words – this makes words less of a mystery and easier to spell.

the	when	become	would
there	which	became	could
their	what	begin	should
they	why	began	
then	while	behind	
them	where	because	
they're			

What's Missing? – Contractions

The word 'contraction' means getting smaller. When looking at contractions in words, one or more letters are missing. When students realize this they know where to put the apostrophe. Play games looking at the missing sounds. Highlight or enlarge the missing sound

I am – I'm	it is – it's	they are – they're	you are – you're
could not – couldn't	she is – she's	will not – won't	

Spoonerisms

Students choose a certain number of list words and write them on strips of paper. The words are then cut in half and rejoined to a different ending. Students swap with a partner and try to guess the original words.

For example:

spel	angle	Original list
chick	ling	spelling
tri	day	chicken
holi	en	triangle
		holiday

Class Activities

Across the Curriculum – Reading Text/Decoding Sound Families

Part of the studies of reading text could be to find sound families. In the text below, words containing "or", "ore", "augh" and "ough" can be listed. Words can be color-coded in "families" and students could add to each list.

Christopher Columbus 1451 – 1506

Christopher Columbus was born in Genoa, Italy, but there is no record of which month he was born in or if he ever lived in Italy. There is evidence that from a very early age he lived in Spain. He learned to read and write in Spanish and he taught himself to read Latin, so he could read geography books. As a young man, he fought for the country of Portugal. In 1465, it is thought that he went to sea and learned to be a sailor. In 1476, he fought in a war for Portugal and when his ship caught fire he swam to shore with the help of an oar.

Portugal was then the westernmost end of the known world and the natural meeting place for sailors who wanted to explore the "new world". People talked about sailing westward, thinking they would eventually reach the East and Cathay (China).

The books Columbus read told him that some astrologers and scientists thought the world was round. They also thought the distance by land between the edge of the west (Spain) and the edge of the east (India) was very long, so the sea distance must be shorter. Many sailors were interested in finding out what was in the west.

The king of Portugal wasn't interested in financing Columbus' voyages, so Columbus went to ask Queen Isabella of Spain. She was very interested, and in 1492, she paid for Columbus to set off and explore the "new world".

The "Santa Maria" sailed from Spain in August 1492 in a small fleet of three ships. Approximately eight weeks later, the crew finally sighted land. They thought it must be east China or the country now known as Japan. It was really one of the Bahama Islands, situated between what we now know as North and South America. During the next three months, Columbus stayed and traveled around these islands. While there he discovered the tobacco plant and decided to take it back to Europe. He also erected crosses all over the islands. The native inhabitants of the islands were afraid of these new people because the sailors took some of them as workers onto the ships. In January 1493, after leaving thirty-eight men on the island with a year's supply of food, stores and ammunition, Columbus began his voyage back to Spain.

About eight weeks later, after battling many fierce storms, Columbus arrived in Spain with lots of stories to tell about the new lands he had discovered.

Class Activities

Word Jumbles

Give letters in alphabetical order and the student has to rearrange according to clues.

For example: television

       eeiilnostv

1. Power is needed
2. We view it
3. It brings the world to us

Students can make up their own Word Jumbles for others in the class to solve.

Add a Word

Each student can add a word to make a word ladder. Have him or her spell it orally first. Use the board or large sheet of paper and permanent markers. If the students want to keep a copy, distribute sheets of paper for them so each student can construct a neat copy.

Examples: "ch", "tch" words

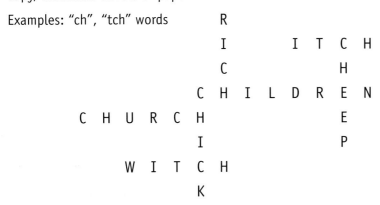

Interest Words

The Fourth of July Words

Choose the word/words you would like to learn this week. Look, say, cover, write, check. Did you get it right? If you did, give yourself a check. If you didn't, try again.

fireworks	July
band	floats
cookout	parade
holiday	picnic
fourth	celebrate
flags	bang
sparklers	flares
firecrackers	decorations
rockets	matches
marching	Uncle Sam

Make up a sentence using your new word.

Can you read the other words?

You may like to try to spell them, too!

How many new words did you learn to spell this week?

Class Activities

Word Sorts

The worksheet sample below can be adapted for use in word sorting activities. Having the students read their own directions for the activity is an excellent way of giving them a purpose for reading. Vary the hints, according to your lesson outcomes.

Spelling Skills and Phonological Awareness

Sort these words into word families according to the sound the letters make. Today, I do not want you to use first letters as a reason for sorting these words. Look carefully for other word families.

(Hint: "ck" – duck, "a" – bath, "ss" – cross, "ou" – cloud, "tt" – cattle, "dd" – fiddle, "pp" – happy, "un" – unlucky)

crack	cricket	unlucky	kiss	house	half
brick	packet	unlock	happy	cross	shout
lock	pocket	pass	puddle	sound	pretty
ticket	chicken	happen	lesson	raft	path
o'clock	rocket	unhappy	slipped	bottom	jetty
knocks	block	pudding	south	mast	basket
track	black	count	happened	bath	cotton
trick	trickery	slipper	mountain	rotten	after
flock	player	thousand	muddle	calf	mask
luck	brick	riddle	mouse	chickens	tricking

- Once you have sorted your words, explain to your partner why you put the words into these particular groups.
- Could you have chosen different groups?
- Discuss your partner's choice of groups.
- Cut and glue your words onto a page in your book and give each of your word family groups a name. Cut and glue carefully.

You may wish to add your own rules to the above list as any become apparent to the class.

Forgetful Syllables

Write part of a word on the chalkboard, leaving out whole syllables. Have students guess the word. Finally, clap out the syllables. See syllable rules on page 18.

____ ____ /happ/i/____ ____ ____   _____ (unhappiness)

for/____ ____ ____ /ate   _____ (fortunate)

auc/____ ____ ____ /eer   _____ (auctioneer)

Class Activities

Sporting Puzzles

In this activity, look at decoding the "k", "er", "o" and long vowel "a" sounds, as well as looking at syllables.

Sort into one-, two- or three-syllable words. Clap or tap out the syllables. See page 18 for syllable rules.

squash, golf

jog/ging, ten/nis, crick/et, foot/ball, sur/fing, sai/ling, base/ball, soc/cer, bas/ket/ball

Across the Curriculum – Writing/Spelling/History

Students could compare what they know about Marco Polo, for example, with what they know about Christopher Columbus. Remember to include who, where, when, what, how and why in planning your information.

Following this activity, students could brainstorm "o" words during language. "Marco Polo" could head the list.

	Marco Polo	Christopher Columbus
Who		
Where		
When		
What		
How		

Research Table

Use this table to record valuable information about things you want to know about; e.g., occupations.

Occupation	What does he/she do?	Where does he/she work?	What/who does he/she help?	What type of job is it?

References that I used in my research: _____

Across the Curriculum – Extracting Information/History

Fill in the table below with information taken from the text read when learning about these explorers.

Explorer	When did he/she live?	Who was he/she?	Where did he/she travel?	Why did he/she explore these places?

Glossary of Terms

Adjectives   are describing words, they give a more exact meaning to a noun

Adverbs   words that give more exact meaning to other words. Adverbs modify verbs, adjectives and other adverbs.

Digraph   two letters used together representing a single speech sound

Nouns   name of a person, place or thing. There are two kinds of nouns, common and proper.

Proper nouns name particular people, places or things so they must have a capital letter.

Common nouns are not capitalized, they can be

- **abstract**   naming qualities actions or ideas like courage, loyalty, kindness
- **concrete**   naming materials we can see or touch like bike, window, house
- **collective:**   naming a group of persons or things like class, team, flock, litter

Phonetic   having to do with speech sounds, indicating pronunciation

Phonics   a method of teaching reading/spelling skills

Prefix   a syllable, syllables or a word put at the beginning of a word to change its meaning or to form a new word.

Pronouns   are substitutes, they take the place of nouns in speech and writing e.g., her, him, he, she, his, hers, it, they, them, you, I, we, us

Root Word   the essential part of a word from which other words are derived

Suffix   an addition made at the end of a word to form another word of different meaning or function

Syllable   a word or part of a word pronounced as a unit, usually consisting of a vowel alone or with one or more consonants

The Nym family

Antonym   a word that means the opposite of another word

Synonym   a word that means the same or has a similar meaning to a word in the same language

Homonym   one of two or more words that are identical in pronunciation or spelling but have a different meaning (sale/sail).

Homographs   a word of the same spelling as another, but a different origin and meaning (bank/bank).

Homophone   having the same sound, the letters "c" and "k" are homophones in "cork"; another word for homonym.

Trigraph   three letters used together representing a single speech sound

Verb   a word that describes an action or a state of being

Notes

Notes

Notes